YOU ARE
SOUL
BEAUTIFUL

YOU ARE SOUL BEAUTIFUL
A Unique Perspective into the Soul's Quest for Its Destiny

2024 Award Winner

PRAISE FOR
You Are Soul Beautiful

"Bravo to Connie Fusella for sharing this captivating and inspiring masterpiece. Using incredibly inspiring recounts of her own life story, Fusella unlocks timeless wisdom of the soul and offers lessons that are sure to expand your mind and consciousness beyond the constructs of this 3D reality. Written with profound insight and deep compassion, *You are Soul Beautiful* is more than just another spiritual book. It is a glimpse into eternity, a peek beyond the veil and a healing kiss from the Universe. A must read for anyone who is willing to remember who they truly are."

> —Kim Russo, The Happy Medium, Certified Psychic Medium,
> TV Host and author of *The Happy Medium: Life Lessons From the Other Side* and *Your Soul Purpose: Learn How to Access the Light Within*

"In *You are Soul Beautiful,* Connie Fusella brings the reader on a journey with her. In it, she shares the story of her coming to understand and embrace her psychic, intuitive and mediumistic abilities—in order to fully honor her true soul purpose. In reading her story, the reader is invited into the knowing that we each have a beautiful soul purpose—and it is there, waiting for each of us to explore!"

> —Laura Lynne Jackson, NY Times Bestselling author of *Signs: The Secret Language of the Universe* and *The Light Between Us*

"*You Are Soul Beautiful* is a riveting account of a fascinating story taking the reader into the mind of a medium as you share the discovery process of spiritual awakening. A revelatory tale; an inside look at mediumship, near-death experiences, past life regression, signs and psychic phenomena. I couldn't put it down."

> —Tom Gould, Co-host of The Gathering on Signs of Life Radio

YOU ARE SOUL BEAUTIFUL

A Unique Perspective into the
Soul's Quest for its Destiny

CONNIE FUSELLA

Certified Psychic Medium

STELLA BRILLANTE PUBLISHING

Palm Coast, Florida

Dedicated to the loving memory of my parents, Marianne and Salvatore Trocino, for instilling in me a strong moral and ethical compass to keep me grounded and humble. Together you inspired me in vastly different ways to reach for the stars and become the person that I am today. Neither of you had the chance to witness my work as a psychic medium before transitioning to the Afterlife, and I hope that as you watch over and guide me, that I continue to make you proud every day. I love and miss you both immensely.

And to my amazing sons, Nicholas and Anthony, you are the lights and loves of my life and without a doubt my greatest accomplishments. Watching you both grow into extraordinary young gentlemen has brought me such pride and joy, and I know you will always shine brightly.

And to my wonderful husband, Nick, for your love and ongoing support on this journey. Thank you for always believing in me and trusting in my spiritual path.

And most importantly, my eternal gratitude to Spirit for always showing up and keeping me on my continuous evolving path of Light. I pray that you will always keep me humble, grateful, and faithful in service to the beautiful souls in Spirit and those still present in need of comfort, healing, and closure from experiencing the loss of loved ones.

Table of Contents

Foreword xi
Introduction 1

Chapter 1: The Soulitudes 7

Chapter 2: Not So Ordinary Beginning 19

Chapter 3: The Mysterious Old Man in the Basement 29

Chapter 4: Lea the Lion 33

Chapter 5: On the Wings of a Butterfly 37

Chapter 6: The Isis Connection 41

Chapter 7: Near-Death Experience #1 My Life Review 47

Chapter 8: Near-Death Experience #2
            Through the Tunnel and into the Glow 53

Chapter 9: The Metaphysical Pull 59

Chapter 10: Flying and Floating 63

Chapter 11: Robert, An Angel Among Us 67

Chapter 12: My First Premonition—Touched by an Angel 73

Chapter 13: Near-Death Experience #3 Meeting Jesus 77

Chapter 14: Reading Tarot Cards Came as a Shock to Me 79

Chapter 15: Jacob, My Spirit Guide 83

Chapter 16: I am a Medium 87

Chapter 17: White Noise Vibration 91

Chapter 18: 444 95

Chapter 19: Forever Family Foundation 101

Chapter 20: Signs... 105

Chapter 21: The Past, Present and Future Me...................111

Chapter 22: Clear at Last....................................117

Epilogue 121

Acknowledgements.. 123

About the Author.. 125

Foreword

Having worked closely with mediums (people that demonstrate the ability to communicate with discarnate entities) over the past twenty years, I am always interested in learning about their childhood. Since most evidential mediums report intuitive abilities as a child, how they dealt with these gifts is often fascinating. Most mediums describe such childhood experiences as occurring without fear but prompting great curiosity. Children are most often blank slates, not yet conditioned by social norms, and therefore simply experience rather than judge.

Connie saw a mysterious figure hanging around her basement, and that was met by initial fear, but there was a reason. Her dad admonished her that there was a monster in one part of the basement. His imaginary caution was well intentioned, as he wanted her to stay away from injury due to contact with hot pipes in the furnace room. Naturally, she believed that she was seeing this monster, which was not a pleasant experience, but she then became accepting of this non-traditional home resident.

Many mediums tend to compartmentalize or suppress their childhood encounters with non-physical beings. Parents are usually not accepting of such tales and summarily dismiss them. It is usually in the later years when such abilities surge to the forefront, and the medium must make a choice as to whether they want to embrace this gift or continue to ignore it. As was the case with Connie, a series of synchronistic events usually provide the impetus, with the urging of Spirit, to act upon and further develop their abilities. This decision is never an easy one to make, as it flies in the face of materialist thinking, and opens one up to labeling, judgment, and even ridicule. We don't often think of mediums as being brave, but taking such a leap is an act of courage.

A question that is often asked is, "Why don't mediums ever provide descriptions of what the afterlife is like?" My answer is that the primary goal of a person in the Spirit realm is to let their loved ones know that they still exist. Period. This can only be done by providing specific evidence that the sitter (the person getting the reading) will understand. The mediumship process is not a direct telephone line to another dimension. It is not an easy task for a medium to receive telepathic communication, put it into words, and translate for the sitter. That is difficult enough, let alone long descriptive narratives about the next world.

However, Connie is in a unique position, as she has had three near death experiences. She has seen the Other Side, something that not many mediums can claim. Each experience provided different layers of knowledge and insights, which now make her better able to understand messages now communicated from another dimension.

Historical channeled accounts, communicated mostly by mediums who went into trance, provide descriptions of different spheres or dimensions in the non-physical world. In this book, Connie has taken a different twist as she describes Soulitudes, which are categories that people fall into in the physical realm. It is her hope that, by examining these categories, we can better understand our soul's path and destiny. It is a unique approach to the recognition that we are mere fragments of a greater soul that is always looking to grow.

Throughout the book, Connie goes into detail about her life, often recounting humorous anecdotes, emotional and physical trauma, and signs from Spirit. It is an interesting peek into the joys and travails of one dedicated to helping others. Connie's mediumistic abilities have been verified, under controlled conditions, by Forever Family Foundation's Medium Evaluation Certification Process. She is the real deal, and the information in this book can be trusted.

Bob Ginsberg
Co-Founder Forever Family Foundation
Author of *The Medium Explosion: A Guide to Navigating the World of Those Who Claim to Communicate with the Dead* and *My Life: Here and There*

Introduction

Welcome Beautiful Souls! If you are reading this book, know the Universe has conspired to lead you here. The idea of authoring a book illustrating my personal experiences and soul's quest to become a psychic medium had been on my mind for the last few years, but somehow the timing just never seemed right.

On more than one occasion, determined to get the book started, I would set aside quiet time and begin writing, but inevitably each time I would get distracted, go in a different direction, or become frustrated and decide to put it aside for another day. I have come to learn and understand the way the Universe works through the many life lessons that I have experienced and know that everything happens when it is supposed to happen versus when we would like it to occur. Without a doubt, this has truly been one of my life's hardest lessons to accept and I have had to learn to slow my pace down and let things happen organically and naturally versus hyper focusing, stressing, and trying to control every aspect of my life. This is not something that comes easy for me as unfortunately patience is not one of the virtues I was blessed with, so I will always need to put in the effort to continually work on this. Now that I have completed authoring my book, I understand the reason for the delay and why the previous attempts to author my book were constantly thwarted.

I do acknowledge that like so many others who have had to juggle priorities, the last ten years have been a whirlwind for me with having to manage a full-time job, family obligations, and growing my psychic mediumship practice. In addition to all of that, I became the caretaker for both of my parents who were both seriously declining in health and frequently in and out of doctor appointments, hospitals, and rehabilitation facilities.

The loss of my mother in November 2022, reemphasized the importance of spending quality time with family and was the inspiration for making plans for a much needed and long-awaited vacation with my husband and children. I realized that the last family vacation we enjoyed together with my parents before they became too ill to travel was a cruise in March 2015. Too much time had gone by, and I made a resolution to focus on more family quality time because our lives here are too precious and short.

In January 2023, I attended a Grief Retreat in Fort Myers, Florida, as one of the guest certified mediums affiliated with Forever Family Foundation. There, I had the pleasure of getting to know one of my fellow certified medium colleagues, Laura Lynne Jackson, and we agreed to exchange readings at some point in the future.

Months later, on May 2, 2023, my reading with Laura took place and it proved to be very profound and evidential. Laura connected with both of my deceased parents and brought through specific details about their personalities, appearance, unique characteristics, and favorite memories. She also relayed information from my father regarding future events for my children and my career, some of which have already come to fruition.

Another highly evidential component of the reading is the fact that Laura knew that I would author two books and that Spirit would lend their support in getting this accomplished. She also stated that Spirit would convey two key chapters of my first book while I was on a ship. At the time of the reading, Laura had no prior knowledge of my plans to author a book nor was she aware that I was leaving in a couple of weeks on a family cruise to Israel,

Türkiye, and Greece. Laura's reading was completely validated because just as she stated, my Spirit Guides, who I shall refer to as my Spirit Team, started downloading content for this book into my consciousness when I was on the cruise ship.

To be exact, it was the second day of the cruise when I had finally started to unwind after two full hectic travel days on planes, trains, and automobiles. It was still early morning and my husband had already left for the gym and our children were still sleeping, so I headed out of our cabin, grabbed a cappuccino, and settled into a lounge chair on the outer deck gazing out at the serene turquoise ocean. The ship's deck was quiet and still empty as vacationers were either still sleeping or enjoying an early breakfast in one of the main dining rooms. I sat there relishing the peace and quiet, enjoying the slight cool breeze on my face and listening to nothing but the sound of the ocean. It had been a long time since I could just be still and unwind and I felt an overwhelming sense of gratitude for the tranquil experience. My ever-working monkey brain was at peace and that is when my Spirit Team began downloading information about this book into my consciousness. Out of nowhere, I began to hear them relaying information and giving me insight regarding my book's content.

Surprised and excited, and not wanting to disrupt the steady flow of information that Spirit was downloading into my consciousness, I fervently began taking notes on my iPhone as I listened for their guidance. My Spirit Team made me aware that I was still in the learning and discovery phase of who I really was on a soul level and that while drafting my book, I would begin to understand and discover my true destiny. This, my Spirit Team explained, was the reason for the previous delays I experienced when trying to start writing, as certain people, circumstances and events needed to be placed in motion as part of my discovery process that would pertain to the book's content.

When I first began entertaining the idea of authoring a book, my initial plan was to write explicitly about my own spiritual journey, and my Spirit Team conveyed that they still wanted me to proceed in this manner, but with a little twist. They began to impart knowledge about the soul's evolution, and I was shown that our soul progression level is determined by our ability to recognize, accept, achieve, or disregard our true path and purpose, in other words, our human free will to choose our path forward. My Spirit Team gave me direction to provide context, education and information that would resonate with any reader, irrespective of culture or religious belief system, regarding the many ways we respond to our soul's destiny. Per my Spirit Team's instruction, I have broken down these various states of awareness or attitudes towards discovering our true destiny into five levels of soul progression referred to as "The Soulitudes."

We all navigate through The Soulitudes differently, progressing or digressing from one to another, learning lessons and having experiences until we have understood our soul's true purpose. It is also possible and common to stay in one Soulitude or be in two Soulitudes simultaneously during our human experience. To put this into perspective, my Spirit Team asked that I use my own firsthand experiences and spiritual journey to illustrate how my thoughts, actions and circumstances affected my soul's progression through The Soulitudes in search of my true destiny.

We are all beautiful souls here on Earth having a human experience. We are all intuitive beings experiencing instances throughout our lives where we feel a strong gravitational pull towards a person, place, animal, or vocation. How often have you listened to your gut feelings and felt pulled towards things that resonate or bring joy into your life without knowing where those feelings initiated from? Know your beautiful soul is guiding you from your very first to the very last breath you take.

My hope is that as you learn about The Soulitudes and come to know me, through my spiritual quest for my true destiny, that you will come to better understand your own soul's journey by reflecting on the various events, signs and synchronicities that guided you to become the person you are today or perhaps the person that you are striving to become.

Always remember…You Are Soul Beautiful!

CHAPTER 1

The "Soulitudes"

My understanding is that we all have a predestined contract to come into this world as beautiful souls and adorn human bodies to learn lessons of love and enlightenment. Before we have even begun our human spiritual journey, our soul knows and understands what is required to fulfill our predestined soul contract. From the moment we are born, our soul sets out on its quest to guide us in remembering our destiny. It is our free will or attitude, the choices we make and the actions we take that determine whether these predestined soul contracts will be fulfilled.

Some individuals may be extremely fortunate and achieve the desired level of soul evolution during our first human experience and consequently, upon transitioning, join the other souls at the source in Heaven, or whatever your personal belief system recognizes as the Afterlife. We all have the choice to remain with the collective souls, reincarnate as another being or further our soul evolution in the Afterlife by having a job such as mentor or Spirit Guide. Others may partially fulfill or may not succeed at all in fulfilling their soul contract and may then choose to reincarnate for another human experience and chance at enlightenment or their true purpose may be to assist with someone else's soul progression. Again, this is my belief system based on the information communicated to me by my Spirit Team.

I have broken down the ability to recognize the signs and meaningful messages from our souls into five distinct levels of soul progression. These five soul levels depict our awareness, understanding, ability and willingness to accept our soul's guidance to put us on the right path in tandem with how we choose to manage any deterring circumstances, obstacles, or influences that may prohibit the ability to move forward in soul progression such as environment, mental or physical disabilities, addictions, financial constraints, religious beliefs, etc. I refer to these five levels of soul progression as "The Soulitudes" and they are: 1) The Clear, 2) The Confused, 3) The Compromised 4) The Closed and 5) The Committed.

We will all experience The Soulitudes in diverse ways. You may stay in the same Soulitude throughout your lifetime, be in two Soulitudes simultaneously, or more commonly transfer from one Soulitude to another, either progressing towards your soul's true destiny or digressing in soul level. If you digress into another Soulitude, your soul will attempt to guide you back to The Clear Soulitude so you can honor your predestined soul contract before transitioning to the Afterlife.

To help you understand this a little bit better, I have provided an explanation and characteristics for each of The Soulitudes and will illustrate how you can progress or digress from one Soulitude to another by sharing my own spiritual quest to find my soul's destiny.

1. **The Clear Soulitude:** This Soulitude is where our beautiful souls begin, and we should make every effort to remain at this soul level during our human experience. Our predestined purpose for our lives is imprinted on our soul and on some level of our consciousness, we understand what it is that we have agreed to in our soul contract. Some

individuals are fortunate to recognize their purpose or calling early on in life and stay true and unwavering on their soul's journey. This rings true for individuals that are born with unique natural gifts and talents, as their soul's purpose is obvious and made clear to them. Child prodigies that are natural born artists, singers, or musicians may fall into The Clear Soulitude. Take Mozart for example, who started playing songs on the harpsichord at four years old and composing music and performing for royal audiences when he was only six years old. The Clear have been doing what they love from an early age and continue to be successful at it as adults. The key to The Clear is that they are aware and mindful of their true purpose and are open to recognizing and following their soul's messages and signs. They are the fortunate individuals that quickly discover what brings their soul joy and naturally gravitate on the path that was meant for them, taking the initiative to overcome any obstacles to stay true to their calling or destiny and remain at The Clear Soulitude.

2. **The Confused Soulitude:** The vast majority of individuals fall into this soul level due to the numerous ways in which someone can experience The Confused Soulitude. These individuals may not be aware of their path right away, in which case, the Universe in tandem with your soul sends signs and ensures that we experience life events deemed necessary to realize our true purpose. The Confused may be receiving signs but do not recognize them or know how to interpret them. This could be a result of their own lack of education, frame of reference, religious beliefs, or other constraint. How many people do you know that have struggled to figure out what their purpose is, changing

course in their education, occupation, relationships, and even spiritual beliefs until they finally find what resonates with them? The Confused are trying to find their soul's true purpose but don't know where to begin and their efforts are usually associated with experiencing necessary failures and even heartbreak as they try to figure it out. For instance, someone may need to experience the unconditional love of a family member or pet and then experience their loss to inspire a passion that navigates them to their soul's true destiny of becoming a physician or veterinarian. Another trait of The Confused is misinterpreting an experience as a fated occurrence leading to downstream problems. For example, remaining in a relationship because a strange circumstance brought you and your partner together and therefore you consider it to be a fated match or destiny, even though your partner has negative or toxic proclivities. We need to be able to discern when random occurrences are in fact fated and for our highest good versus simply just being random occurrences with no bearing on our true path forward. Another trait of The Confused is ignoring what makes their soul happy and choosing what is familiar or easy to them. They may choose to follow in their parents' footsteps, whether it be working in the same industry, attending the same college, or even residing in the same location. There is, of course, nothing wrong with this notion but it may not be the right path. Following in our parents' footsteps is what I believe to be the path of least resistance, meaning that we take the road that we are familiar with because we can see firsthand how it worked out for our parents, therefore mitigating potential risk. There is a level of comfort knowing expected outcomes and even though this may yield an incredibly happy and productive life, some individuals will be left with feelings of unfulfillment because they are not realizing their soul's true destiny. The Confused may gravitate towards the path that they should follow, but do not understand how to get there as they are still working things out or may need some more convincing. I genuinely believe, coming from the perspective of experiencing The Confused Soulitude firsthand for years, that the Universe and your soul will continue to send signs or life "jolts" if you will, to wake us up to better see the path that was meant for us. Of course, we all have free will to either follow our soul's messages or continue to ignore them, but if it is your calling, your soul will keep calling.

3. **The Compromised Soulitude:** This group of individuals consists of those that have done the work necessary for their soul's evolution and have realized their soul's destiny, but a variety of factors prevent them from moving forward into The Clear Soulitude. Obstacles, circumstances, or deterrents that come into play are financial resources, relationships, family obligations, religious beliefs, physical location, education, and physical, emotional, or mental well-being. Someone in The Compromised Soulitude knows what they want and should do but they are unable to progress forward because of a constraint, for example, they are unable to leave their current career or situation that affords them financial stability. Sometimes individuals in The Compromised Soulitude are held back by the needs of others, whether it be raising children, taking care of parents, or they are in a relationship that requires their full attention and does not allow for time for their personal spiritual growth. Individuals can also fall into The Compromised

Soulitude due to feelings of low self-esteem and negative perceptions regarding their capabilities thus holding themselves back from progressing to The Clear Soulitude because they do not believe enough in themselves. If you allow yourself to be open to your soul's destiny, then the Universe will guide you to it, doing so in the time period that your soul deems appropriate. Everything happens for a reason and even though we may think we are ready to embark on our true path, our soul may need to further evolve and experience more lessons and spiritual growth. The Universe may put obstacles in your path that may seem like difficult lessons, but they are in fact blessings that will lead you to a better place. Trust the organic unfoldment of your soul's journey.

4. **The Closed Soulitude:** Some individuals struggle to open themselves up to see the signs from their soul or simply choose to ignore them. These unfortunate individuals are experiencing unfulfilling lives because they are simply not doing what makes their soul happy. I am sure you have met people who constantly change jobs, never stay in one place too long and never land in a position that compliments their skills or abilities, all leading to failure. They are never satisfied with their careers and always make up excuses for their discontent. Individuals experiencing The Closed Soulitude often have unsuccessful or dysfunctional relationships, always placing the blame on the other person for the failure. Alternatively, they may be at The Closed Soulitude because they truly are a victim due to another's negative influence over them and they do not have the wherewithal to break free from their situation to find a better path forward. Individuals

experiencing The Closed Soulitude may have digressed from The Confused Soulitude by continually missing or choosing to ignore their soul's guidance whether it be because of their ego, denial, or other negative influence (their own or others around them) that impairs judgement or rationale (i.e., substance, emotional, or physical abuse or mental impairment). The Closed always see the glass half empty instead of half full and exude negative energy via their thoughts, words, and actions. These individuals can be found on both sides of the spectrum, those that think too much of themselves and have a false sense of who they are and how they are perceived (ego) or alternatively, think too little of themselves due to unfulfilling or negative influences or experiences. They are often "victims" and attach themselves to others that are in the same situation or to someone who will enable them because they refuse to do the much-needed inner growth and self-reflecting analyses needed for their soul to progress. The Closed are at low vibration spiritually making it difficult to receive the signs and guidance their soul is sending to help them move out of this Soulitude. Individuals in The Closed Soulitude need to do the personal work in removing negative people, habits, and situations from their lives to facilitate their soul's evolution. They truly exhibit the human struggle to achieve enlightenment and free will to choose between a positive or negative existence.

5. **The Committed Soulitude:** Simply put, these are the individuals who have agreed to a predestined soul contract to experience a challenging, painful, or short-lived human life with the purpose of learning valuable life lessons to further their own soul's evolution or to assist in the progression of

someone else's soul level. Even though The Committed can exercise their free will to move out of this Soulitude, many remain steadfast to their soul contract commitment. The Committed often fall into this Soulitude after transitioning into the Afterlife and having a Life Review revealing their shortcomings during their human experience. With this knowledge, they agree to reincarnate into The Committed Soulitude for another chance to make amends and reach enlightenment for themselves or others. This Soulitude is the one that really tests our faith and makes us skeptical of the working order of the Universe or the God you believe in by making us ask those hard questions such as: What possible good could come from this? Why did this have to happen? What kind of God would allow this? Many of The Committed are the young children and loved ones that have passed too soon from terminal illness, random accidents, suicide, or acts of violence or hatred. At a point in time, these individuals made a soul agreement to live a challenging life no matter how inconceivable that may seem to us. These deaths leave a long-lasting impression on us, challenge our belief systems, and may lead to feelings of resentment or anger. These are human feelings that are common and understandable because as humans we cannot even possibly pretend to understand how someone would agree to this type of soul agreement. It is only upon transitioning to the Afterlife that we become spiritually equipped with the knowledge of soul contracts and can fully understand and accept the purpose of The Committed Soulitude.

June 26, 2023—Reading Session

It was a typical beautiful sunny afternoon in Parrish, Florida, and Leslie Singleton and her twin daughters, Ashley and Mia, arrived at my home office for their reading session. As they busied themselves getting comfortable and setting up their iPhones to record the session, I asked them how they had come to hear about me. Leslie stated that she recently attended one of my local group demonstration events and it left her curious, inspired, and eager to schedule a private session.

Her daughters had never experienced a psychic medium reading and I sensed that they were a bit apprehensive. Per my usual protocol, I put my clients at ease and explained that there was nothing to be nervous about and assured them that they were in a safe place. I made them aware that as a medium, I do not control the spirits that come through in the reading sessions, but it has been my experience that the loved ones they are hoping to hear from do make themselves known through meaningful evidence. I instructed everyone to put their intentions out by asking their loved ones to join us for the reading session and let them know that I was doing the same.

I took deep breaths and then began to scribble on a blank notepad used for writing down images or information that Spirit relays to me during private reading sessions. Immediately, I sensed the family's loved ones drawing closer and wrote down the words "male, father, military, heart attack, under seventy years old" and asked Leslie if she understood a father figure in Spirit with a military connection that had died from a heart attack before he turned seventy. Leslie validated this information stating that her father was a Marine and died of a heart attack in his late sixties. The reading was off to a good start, and I continued to bring through more evidence relating to her father including his physical description and significant months for birthdays, anniversaries and passings. Then I sensed another younger gentleman drawing close, knowing that his passing was sudden, and he did not have time to say good-bye to his loved ones. I heard the name "John." I asked my clients, "Do you understand a younger male who passed unexpectedly under the age of sixty due to an accident with a connection to the name John?" Ashley validated that John was her father's younger brother who passed unexpectedly in a car accident. As Ashley spoke, I felt the loving energy of her father come forward and surround both her and her twin sister, Mia, who was sitting beside her. I knew that he was the reason for this family to be here today. I turned to the mother, Leslie, and asked if she lost a husband in the last year and she confirmed her husband passed about six months ago. An image of Thomas the Train flashed before me, which is my symbol for the name "Thomas." I asked if they understood that name and received validation that the gentlemen's name was in fact Thomas, but he preferred to be called Tom. As Tom, drew nearer to me, I sensed he had a tough battle with an overall physically debilitating medical condition. He also showed me my sign indicating that his illness had caused him to become bedridden. Tom wanted to thank his whole family for the group effort in the exceptional care they provided which enabled him to stay in the home where he eventually passed. Tom also mentioned that someone in the family with a medical background was instrumental in taking extremely diligent care of him. The family confirmed that Tom fought a battle with ALS, and he was bedridden and cared for by the family in the home, especially by Ashley who was a registered nurse.

Tom continued relaying evidential information. "He is happy about the change you made to the home and likes that it is much brighter now with white walls and light-colored furniture. Do you understand this?" I asked. Leslie started to cry and explained that she had just bought a new home with freshly painted white walls and also purchased all new light-colored furniture and decorations. She had been distraught over selling the condominium that she and Tom had lived in for so long and hearing that he was pleased with her decision was a huge comfort for her.

Next, I heard the word "Blackjack." "Why would I hear "Blackjack"? I asked and Mia shouted out, "that was the name of our dog that passed last year, he was our father's buddy!" I smiled and said "Well, you should know then that Blackjack is keeping your father company." As I was talking my hand had been drawing a heart with wings, so I held up my notepad and asked about the significance of the symbol. Ashley stated that after her father passed away, a friend had given her a necklace with the word 'DAD' engraved on a heart with wings which looked just like my sketch. Tom showed me images of him riding a bicycle to the beach and then sitting in the sun, relaxing, and doing crossword puzzles. Leslie confirmed that these were all things her husband loved to do. Tom went on to give more evidence pertaining to himself and family to let them know he was a still a strong presence in their lives.

The family graciously thanked me for giving them peace of mind and assurance that their loved ones were still around them, and I in turn, thanked Spirit for coming through for this lovely family with such strong and meaningful evidence.

As I waved goodbye, I thought to myself...the intelligence of Spirit never ceases to amaze me. Every reading is a unique experience and special in its own way and I am constantly learning from Spirit. I am so grateful to be able to witness and assist in the transformational healing from grief that occurs through delivering meaningful and evidential messages from the Other Side validating that the bonds of love are eternal and can never be broken.

Then I laughed aloud thinking about my long spiritual journey, and despite missing and not understanding many signs from the Universe, my soul persisted and finally succeeded in getting me to realize my true destiny. Looking back to the earlier stages of my life, if someone told me that someday I would become a psychic medium, I would definitely think that they were insane! Nevertheless, I am living proof that if it is your true calling, your soul will keep calling.

It is time to share my story, and so I will start from the not so ordinary beginning...

CHAPTER 2

Not So Ordinary Beginning

I used to think that there was nothing remarkable about my childhood, and that is mostly true. I was born into an old-fashioned Italian family and was fortunate to be raised and loved by my hard-working parents, who instilled in me a strong moral foundation and sense of pride in family values and traditions.

Born and raised in Upstate New York in the small town of Wappingers Falls which is about two hours north of New York City, I grew up experiencing the beautiful fall colors, frigid winters, and the unbearably hot summers that the Hudson Valley is known for. My father immigrated to this country from Calabria, Italy, turning twenty-one as he crossed the ocean on a Greek ship that brought him to Ellis Island, New York. He came with nothing but the clothes on his back, a fourth-grade education, and high hopes for a better life in America, but not being able to speak English together with limited reading and writing skills, the only work he ever knew was hard labor. My father never lost his thick Italian accent and never learned to speak English correctly as he suffered hearing loss from one of his first jobs working in a rock quarry exposing him to frequent dynamite blasting. His hard work and perseverance eventually paid off and about twenty years after he came to this country he started his own successful blacktop construction business with his brothers.

My mother was a native of the small town of New Hamburg, nestled along the Hudson River and known for the train station which was right next to the home she grew up in. When she married my father, she literally moved up the hill to Wappingers Falls. My mother was a high school graduate and worked as a legal secretary until she retired. She also did the bookkeeping for my father's blacktop business.

Our small cape-code style house was always painted some shade of blue for as long as I can remember because it was my mother's favorite color. Mature maple and evergreen trees could be found in the front and side yards, but it was the backyard and specifically the woods beyond it where I spent a lot of time playing during my early childhood years. The small neighborhood I grew up in was known as "Riverview" because in the wintertime when the trees were bare, you could see the Hudson River in the distance below. Most of my relatives lived in the city of Poughkeepsie, so our rural home with a pool became the backyard barbecue destination place for holidays and celebrations. Both sides of the family and neighborhood friends would come together bringing enough food to feed an army, which never went to waste, due to the number of people that attended. My fondest childhood memories are of playing Marco Polo in the pool or croquet, badminton, and volleyball on the lawn with my younger brother, cousins, and neighborhood friends.

Beyond the chain link fence in the backyard was a densely wooded area that divided Riverview and the town of New Hamburg. The woods stretched for miles to eventually border the Hudson River. Being a husky child and very much a tomboy by nature, I spent a lot of time with my best friend, Danielle, in those woods building forts with various tools that I would sneak out of my father's tool chest. We were the only two girls in the neighborhood that played in the woods with the other boys so there were times that we had to defend our forts from a hostile takeover. This was the only time in my life when my chubbiness worked to my advantage, for being much bigger than most of the boys in the neighborhood made me intimidating and difficult to push around. By default, my bulky build led to me assuming the role of Danielle's guardian and protector since she was a pretty and petite girl. It did not take me long to realize that some of the neighborhood boys had silly crushes on Danielle and being very clever and already having an entrepreneurial mind, I used this knowledge to make money. With Danielle's permission, I started charging the boys twenty-five cents for a quick kiss on her cheek. When we accumulated a dollar fifty, Danielle and I would ride our bikes to the corner deli and treat ourselves to an Italian sub or meatball hero. Danielle thought I was a genius.

When the neighborhood boys were amicable, we would all play Lost in Space or pretend we were on a safari looking for wild creatures in the forest. But my favorite time was when Danielle and I would spend time together in our fort and play our own version of Swiss Family Robinson, pretending to be isolated in the forest instead of on an island. We had make-believe husbands, children, and dogs. I always insisted that my pretend husband was very tall with dark hair and green eyes, and I never deviated from that description which is interesting as most of my family was short to medium height with brown eyes and I had never met anyone with green eyes before. It is probably not a coincidence that my current husband, Nick, is six foot four with dark hair and green eyes. It is one of the many quirky and random things I said, felt or did as a child that came to be true as I grew up and became an adult. Somehow these ideas were imprinted on my soul and in my consciousness and eventually came to fruition.

The inside of our modest house was approximately fifteen hundred square feet with three small bedrooms, one small bathroom and a galley shaped kitchen area that led to a small dining room/living room space. One of my father's good friends was a tile installer so our kitchen and bathroom floors were both covered in a tiny checkerboard pattern of a light pink and gray tile left over from one of his jobs. Our appliances and formica countertops were a matching honey mustard color, a cringe-worthy contrast to the gray and pink floors. When I was in middle school the kitchen area got a fashion upgrade (in my parents' eyes only) in the form of a huge incredibly tacky wallpaper mural of Sorrento Italy on the wall behind the kitchen table. From that moment on, we dined "al fresco" looking at the crystal blue water that stretched out beyond the big Roman stone pillars adorned with bright, fuchsia-colored flowers on huge green leafy vines.

There was an entryway mudroom between the garage and kitchen which housed the doorway that led downstairs to the basement. This tiny mudroom also served as a food pantry, office for my father's blacktop business and the place where at any given time you could find an assortment of shoes, work boots or sneakers piled up along the walls.

Like typical homes in upstate New York, our house had a semi-finished basement which held a multitude of different memories for me as I went through the various stages of my life. The main room was quite large and rectangular and painted in different colors of whatever leftover paint my father could find. The walls were white, yellow, and light blue and accented with support columns painted in a lovely shade of circus peanut orange sorely standing out against the black-flecked vinyl flooring. Surrounding the main room was an L-shaped corridor with an entry door on each end. When you went through the door at the base of the stairs, you would find a small laundry room area to the right. If you turned left, you would have thought you stepped into an Italian salumeria with supersede, salami, and provolone hanging on strings from the ceiling. My father had installed wooden shelves along the corridor for storing mason jars filled with homemade tomato sauce, pickled eggplant, marinated peppers, bottles of homemade wine and stone crocks filled with cracked olives immersed in olive oil.

I didn't dare venture past the shelves and around the bend because my father made it very clear to me from an early age that I was forbidden to go back there or open the door at the far entrance of the corridor because if I did, I would encounter the scary "momo" that lived back there. "Momo" is Calabrian slang for monster. Believing that one lived in the corridor behind that forbidden door instilled a great terror in me and absolutely did the job of preventing me from going exploring in a dangerous area for a child, the furnace room. Fear of encountering the momo lurking in the basement stayed with me for years. As I grew a little older, I vividly remember the trepidation I would feel when my mother asked me to retrieve the laundry or grab a jar of sauce from the basement. I was a big scaredy cat and was afraid to go alone, so I cleverly resorted to enlisting the help of my dog, Queenie, to help with these tasks. Queenie was a stray Sheltie-mix dog that my older cousins had rescued from some mean kids in Poughkeepsie who had tied her up to a fence and were throwing rocks at her. My cousins intervened and rescued Queenie and brought her home but because they lived in the city and did not have a yard suitable for raising a dog, to my delight, she ended up coming to live with us. Queenie was my first pet and my love for rescue dogs began with her. She was extremely smart, and I enlisted her to become my trusty basement scout. Whenever I needed to retrieve something from the basement, I would throw one of Queenie's squeaky toys down the stairs so she would go first. I would wait to see if Queenie sensed anything unusual and if all seemed normal, then I would run down the stairs, grab what I needed as quickly as possible and then dart back up the stairs without looking back. I was afraid that if I moved too slowly, the dreaded momo would get me! I am sure it would be frowned upon in today's world for a parent to scare the heck out of their child by telling them there was a monster in the basement, but those were different times and it definitely deterred me from venturing behind that door and hurting myself in the furnace room.

Aside from the scary momo memories, the basement also provided me with positive cherished memories of family parties and holiday celebrations. When I was little, we hosted Christmas Eve parties, and the basement was adorned with festive decorations and long folding tables were covered with all the traditional Italian Feast of the Seven Fishes dishes, including pasta, antipasto, desserts, and bottles of homemade wine. I would run around playing and dancing to the loud music with my cousins while the grownups celebrated in the bar area. For a couple of years, my Nonno (grandfather) dressed up as Santa Claus and came down the stairs bearing small gifts for all the children. Those were such fun times and great memories.

In my later elementary school days, the basement became the stage for my best friend Danielle and I to let our imaginations run wild. We pretended we were famous singers and would practice our favorite songs and then recruit the neighborhood boys to sing duets with us and put together our version of a Donny and Marie Osmond Variety Show. Still a savvy entrepreneur, I would charge admission fees to the neighborhood kids to come and watch the show and of course all proceeds went to purchasing deli sandwiches and goodies for me and my best friend. We also formed a neighborhood space mission club with the requirements to join being a large contribution of candy that could be easily shared with the group, (candy dots, jellybeans, tootsie rolls) to sustain us on our space missions. Before leaving for every adventure, we would state our mission and then stand to recite the Pledge of Allegiance in front of an American Flag that we stuck in a mason jar filled with marbles. Our imaginations would take us to all sorts of places where we would encounter dangerous aliens and strange creatures who spoke to us in different languages or through mind communication. Somehow, at an incredibly early age, I believed and understood that we were just a tiny part of the Universe and so much more existed beyond our physical presence on earth.

I was an extremely creative child and thankfully Danielle was also imaginative and shared my interest in writing fantastical stories. We would retreat to the basement and write and illustrate stories about magical creatures that we could speak to with our minds and beautiful colored crystals that we would find that gave us special powers like becoming invisible, being able to see in the dark, or grow smaller or bigger in size. Danielle would sit attentively and completely enthralled as I read my stories aloud to her.

Even at this early age, I felt a bit like a fish out of water and somehow instinctively knew that I did not belong in Upstate New York. I hated the cold winters and damp weather and loved warm weather and feeling the sun on my face. When I was in middle school, my family vacationed to Disney World in Orlando, Florida, and I somehow knew for certain that I would end up living in the sunshine state when I grew up. I remember telling Danielle that I was going to live in Florida one day, with my husband, two children and dogs and be a famous author. It was just another one of those quirky things I said or felt as a child that came to fruition.

Later in life, about a couple of years after graduating from high school, I got the notion that I should move out on my own. This was attributed to wanting to move to the city of White Plains, New York, to be closer to my job and eliminate the exhausting one-hour commute in heavy traffic. I found a cute one-bedroom apartment in the second story of an older home owned by a middle-aged professional couple. It was small but conveniently located less than fifteen minutes from my place of employment. I vividly remember the day I moved out, being so excited at the prospect of being out on my own. My father loaded my clothes, boxes, heavy dresser, and childhood bed with the saggy mattress into the back of his pickup truck and drove me to my new apartment. I spent the day unpacking and putting together a list of items that I would need for decorating my new space in my own personal style. The very next day my parents paid me a surprise visit bringing furniture. They presented me with an ugly couch upholstered in rough scratchy material in a tacky mustard, green, blue, and burgundy plaid pattern. It was extremely hideous and definitely not what I had in mind. In addition to the couch being a décor eyesore, it was extremely uncomfortable. My father boasted that the couch was very sturdy and well-made. The cushions and back were unyielding as if they were composed of concrete. I made a mental note to add one large blanket big enough to cover the entire hideous couch and a couple of soft pillows to my list of items that I needed to purchase. The other item my parents surprised me with was a tiny kitchen table with two metal chairs. I admit to not having lots of friends growing up so perhaps my parents took this into consideration when purchasing the little table with two seats. Nothing was going to dampen my excitement about having my own place, and I did not want to appear ungrateful, so I smiled and thanked my parents profusely for their thoughtful gifts.

Despite feeling exhausted from unpacking my belongings and trying to get everything organized, I did not sleep a wink the first night alone in my apartment. Strange noises were coming from outside my bedroom door, and I kept seeing scary shadows on the wall. My imagination was running wild inciting my fear, and I kept telling myself that things would get better as I grew accustomed to this unfamiliar place and all the sounds associated with it. But this was not to be, and sleepless nights became the norm, so it did not take long before I quickly became disenchanted with living on my own. I tried to tough it out and lasted for about two months. Stressed and sleep deprived, I finally had to swallow my pride and tell my parents that I wanted to come home because I was too afraid to sleep in the apartment by myself. My parents were slightly annoyed at the inconvenience of having to move me back home after such a short while. Also, they did not know where to put me as they had wasted no time in converting my bedroom into a den where they could watch television and our small home had no extra bedrooms. My hideous couch found its new home in my parents' den, and I ended up in the basement. The ever-versatile basement now became my bedroom and thankfully, by this time I had outgrown the fear of encountering the momo, so I was sure to get some sleep!

I always thought my childhood was simple and ordinary, however, looking back I have come to realize that at an incredibly early age things started to become a little peculiar. I was exhibiting extrasensory abilities of seeing and hearing Spirit, knowing things I had no other previous way of knowing and predicting future events. I was unaware that these extrasensory perceptions were not typical attributes. I was not brought up in a family or environment that had knowledge of or talked about psychics, mediums, or anything of the metaphysical nature, so I had no frame of reference on these matters. As far as I was concerned, I was just like any other child.

I have provided detailed information about the basement and how throughout my life that area of the house came to mean different things to me. The reason for this is because the basement had a very profound impact on my life. It was in the basement where my first experience with Spirit occurred, and it happened right in front of that ominous forbidden door where the dreaded momo was purported to dwell. The basement is where I discovered the mysterious old man.

CHAPTER 3

The Mysterious Old Man in the Basement

I was about four years old when I first saw him. As a young child I was always clinging to my mother often hanging on her side when she was doing chores around the house, so naturally when she went down to the basement to do the laundry on Saturday mornings, I tagged along right behind her. I always remained close to her side just in case I encountered the scary momo.

One day, this usually non-eventful routine turned out unexpectedly different. Like all the times before, I followed my mother to the basement and sang nursery rhymes while she proceeded with the laundry ritual of loading the dirty clothes into the washer, folding the clean clothes from the dryer, and then piling them into the laundry basket to bring upstairs. This time before taking my first step to ascend the stairs, I sensed something or someone behind me. I remember having this strange sensation and feeling the back of my neck hairs tingling, so I turned to look back over my shoulder. That is when I first saw him...the mysterious old man in the basement! Out of the corner of my eye and just for a fleeting second, I saw him standing on the far side of the main room in front of that door I was forbidden to open and then Poof! he was gone! I was terrified and hurriedly shoved past my mother who was making her way up the stairs and ran straight to my bedroom. I reached for my beloved stuffed animal "Lea" propped up as usual on my pillow and hugged her tight as I pulled the comforter over my head. I stayed like that for a while, eyes closed and clutching Lea under the covers while my heart raced pounding with fear. I was fighting the first thought that ran through my mind which was "had I just seen the dreaded momo that my father had warned about?!" I was distraught at this thought and ran out of my room and straight for my mother and threw my arms around her crying "I just saw the momo downstairs!" My mother gave me a bewildered look and then chuckled and said, "don't be silly, you probably just saw a shadow, there is no momo in the basement!"

After clinging to my mother for a bit, my heart stopped racing and I went back to my room to sit with Lea and reflect on the strange event that I had just experienced. Now I was really confused, was there or was there not a momo dwelling behind that forbidden door in the basement? My father says yes, but my mother says no. This was all too overwhelming for my young mind to process. I was quite sure I saw an old man and he did not fit the description of a scary momo. Maybe the old man was mean and wicked and did terrible things to little children and that is why he was considered a momo. I really wanted to believe my mother and tried to convince myself that I had just seen a shadow. It all happened so suddenly, the mysterious old man was there for just a second and then he vanished. The more I pondered the situation, the more I felt certain that I did not see a momo, but I could not convince myself that I did not see an old man in the basement. He was all too real to be a shadow. My young mind was racing with question after question. Why would an old man be lurking in the basement? How long has he been there? If he was living in the basement, where did he sleep? Why didn't he ever come upstairs and join us for dinner? None of this made any sense to me and I concluded that there could be no other explanation other than my mind must be playing tricks on me and like my mother suggested, I must have seen a shadow. This explanation brought me comfort and I tried not to think about the mysterious old man in the basement anymore.

However, a week later when Saturday morning rolled around and it was laundry time again, my shadow theory would become dispelled. I remember feeling a little apprehensive as we descended the stairs to the basement, so I peered out cautiously from behind my mother, glancing in the direction of the forbidden door where I had seen the old man previously. He was not there. I did a quick room scan—nothing, no one, and feeling relieved, I proceeded with following my mother into the laundry room. When my mother finished washing and folding the clothes and headed up the stairs, I followed close behind her, but I could not resist sneaking a peek back over my shoulder to see if the old man was there. To my surprise, he was, and we stared at each other. I experienced that strange tingling sensation again, like the hairs on my body were standing on edge. This time, I was not really scared, but more curious and perplexed as I struggled to make sense of this peculiar situation. My mother had begun to ascend the stairs and realizing that I was not moving, turned, and called for me to follow. She saw me standing on the bottom stair looking across the room and said, "What are you looking at?" I remained silent and raised my arm and pointed at the mysterious old man standing in front of the forbidden door. She looked in the direction that I was pointing to and said, "there's nothing there, come on," and so I ran up the stairs behind her.

This was all very overwhelming and confusing for me and a million questions were formulating in my mind. Why didn't my mother acknowledge that she saw the mysterious old man? I had no doubt that I absolutely saw him this time. There could be only one reason she did not say anything...the old man must be some kind of secret that I should not know about. I now began to correlate the secret of the old man hiding downstairs with the story of the momo living behind that forbidden door in the basement and convinced myself that my father invented the scary momo story to keep me from opening that door and discovering that the old man lived back there. It all made sense now, or so I thought at that time. Solving the mystery and knowing this secret gave me a sense of comfort and accomplishment. It also made me braver knowing the mysterious old man was not the dreaded momo.

The following Saturday as I descended the stairs behind my mother, I immediately saw the old man and bravely locked eyes with him, waved, and then ran into the laundry room. I had gotten a better look at him this time and remembered thinking he looked old like a grandfather with salt and pepper hair and shoulders slightly hunched forward. He wore dark pants and a long sleeve white dress shirt, which was snug around his chubby belly. I began to look forward to seeing him now on laundry days and it became a game for me.

Over the following couple of months, I only saw the old man a handful of times and he was always standing in front of that forbidden door. I could not understand why he did not move around the room or talk. He just always remained stationary in the same spot. I felt very grown up in deciding to keep my parents' secret and never mentioned the mysterious old man to anyone. When I stopped seeing him, I surmised that he must have gone to live with a different family because he was very hungry and wanted a nice bed to sleep in. I certainly did not understand it at the time, but I know now that this is when I began to see Spirit.

CHAPTER 4

Lea the Lion

Every child has a favorite stuffed animal, doll, or toy that they become extremely attached to. For me, this was a little stuffed animal lion cub, that I named Lea. She came to me on Christmas morning when I was four years old and became my most beloved toy. As a little girl, I never showed any interest in playing with dolls so when I saw the adorable lion cub with big expressive brown eyes perched on top of a wrapped present under the Christmas tree, the animal lover in me came out and my heart leaped with joy. I loved Lea instantly and from that moment, we were inseparable.

Lea became my best friend, listening attentively to my stories and sitting by my side when I sang songs, colored, played board games and watched cartoons. She would even accompany me outside to the backyard swing set sitting on my lap while I tried to swing high enough to reach the clouds in the sky. She accompanied me everywhere and even took trips in the car when we went to visit relatives. When Lea was not in my arms or by my side, she stayed on top of the pillow on my bed, and I cuddled her in my arms every night before drifting off to sleep.

Not too long after the mysterious old man in the basement disappeared, to my surprise, Lea did something utterly amazing. One day while sprawled out on my bedroom floor coloring, Lea, who of course, was sitting next to me began talking. She said, "you are doing a great job staying in the lines." I just stared at Lea in wonder as I realized that I could hear her voice in my head and somehow, we could understand each other without talking. I always knew Lea was an incredibly special toy, but this development took things to a whole new level! She continued to speak at random times and in short spurts offering little pieces of insight or guidance like "your father is about to come home" and then sure enough minutes later, my father would pull into the driveway. When I played memory card match games, she would say "that one" when I moved my hand over the card that I should choose, and upon flipping the card over, it would always be the match so I would win the game. Lea would also tell me who was calling when the phone rang.

Of course, I understand now that my stuffed animal Lea was not talking to me when I was a child and that I had been experiencing hearing Spirit. It is a well-known fact that young children have extrasensory experiences with the Other Side, whether they see or hear Spirit or have an "invisible friend." These extrasensory perceptions are known as the "clairs" from the French word meaning "clear" and they are psychic abilities that correspond with our senses of seeing, hearing, knowing, feeling, smelling, and tasting. As a young child, I started out clear seeing or clairvoyant, with having seen the Spirit of the mysterious old man in my basement. That experience was a bit overwhelming for my young mind to process and so Spirit intelligently changed the way they communicated with me by making me clear hearing or clairaudient. Receiving spirit communication via clairaudience, made me feel safe and comfortable, believing that I was communicating with my beloved toy lion cub, Lea. It was a much better received and less intimidating experience for me than communicating with a strange old man that I did not know. In the span of less than two years, I was experiencing both clairvoyance and clairaudience abilities, and then I began elementary school, and my brain shifted its focus to the left-brain functions of learning (reading, writing, mathematics), and I stopped hearing Lea.

Like everyone else, I came into this world in The Clear Soulitude. I am a natural born medium, and my soul recognized its true purpose at a very young age when I started exhibiting clairvoyant and clairaudient extrasensory abilities. Understandably, at this youthful age and point of my spiritual journey, I was unable to understand my abilities or the purpose of being able to communicate with Spirit. For this reason, I transitioned into The Confused Soulitude, where I would remain for almost half of my life, struggling to understand my soul's destiny of embracing and sharing my extrasensory gifts in a life of service to both the living and the dead.

CHAPTER 5

On the Wings of a Butterfly

School was always extremely easy for me because even though I stopped seeing and hearing Spirit when I started first grade, another clair or psychic ability emerged more strongly for me, and I was experiencing an uncanny ability to just know things. Claircognizance or clear knowing is a feeling of knowing things without knowing how you know them. This knowing enabled me to absorb and remember information quickly and know answers to questions instantly without thinking. Claircognizance assisted me in achieving mostly straight A's on my report cards from first grade through high school graduation. During the entire time I attended school, I never had to study for a test.

Besides being smart, I also possessed a highly active imagination. I vividly remember one day in fourth grade when Sister Patricia randomly handed out colorful stickers to everyone in the class. I glanced to my left and saw that Travis received a bright red fire truck, and to my right Jeannie received a cute green frog with its tongue sticking out like it was ready to catch a fly. I received a beautiful purple and yellow butterfly. Once all of my classmates received their stickers, Sister Patricia explained that our assignment was to compose an essay about our stickers. I glanced at my beautiful butterfly sticker and began to write away with ease.

Days later my mother received a phone call from the school secretary stating that my teacher, Sister Patricia, wanted to have a discussion. My mother confronted me and demanded to know what I had done to warrant a call from my teacher. For the life of me I could not think of anything that I had done wrong, but then a sense of dread came over me. I was a chubby child and as I got older and heavier, the kids became meaner. At this stage of my life, my mother had to seek out a professional tailor to make the required Catholic school uniform for me because I was too large for the standard offered sizes. This meant that while all the other girls sported the standard dark green, black, and grey plaid skirt with a white blouse and dark green vest uniform, I wore a slightly contrasting color one-piece plaid loose smock making me stick out like a large sore thumb. The boys in my class were mean and teased me relentlessly about my weight, especially during recess time in the parking lot where they could call me names out of earshot range from the nuns. I had grown accustomed to their teasing and bullying but the week of the essay, Billy Manning took it a step further. Billy had written a terrible poem on a small piece of paper that he handed to me at recess as we were forming our line by height order to go back into the classroom. I read the words silently in shame "roses are red, violets are blue, I never saw anyone as fat as you." I quickly wiped the streaming tears from my eyes and crumbled up the note and shoved it into my smock pocket. When we got into the classroom, I threw it in the waste basket behind Sister Patricia's desk. Now, I began to panic wondering if Sister Patricia had found that terrible note. Obviously, she would know that note was meant for me as I was the only overweight child in the class and quite frankly in the whole school. I had never told my parents about my classmates bullying me, so I was mortified at the thought of them finding out which would be even more humiliating for me. I was in a state of turmoil and had to decide if I should say something to my mother to get ahead of the situation or just wait to see what transpires after the phone call. I decided to wait, which turned out to be the right decision, because Sister Patricia's call turned out to be pleasant surprise. She was extremely impressed with how descriptive and well-written my butterfly essay was for a fourth grader. She expressed that my writing skills and vocabulary were at the level of a middle school student and commended me for writing a fantasy story that seemed very real. My mother was pleased with Sister Patricia's high praise, and I secretly felt relieved that the bullying situation was not revealed.

After the call, my mother asked me to tell her about my essay. I explained that my story was about a beautiful butterfly that landed on my arm while playing outside one day. The butterfly quickly became my friend, and we could communicate through our thoughts. The butterfly was magical and grew big enough for me to climb on its back and take me on adventures all over the world. My favorite place that the butterfly took me to visit was a very colorful field with bright flowers and a bright golden sun. In that magical place I would laugh, sing, dance and play with the other children who lived there. In my essay, I wrote about how everyone in this place was beautiful, kind, and happy and how I felt very loved and safe. When I finished explaining my essay, my mother told me that she was very proud of me and impressed with my make-believe story.

Sister Patricia's phone call and my mother's praise left me confused because I really did not understand why they were making such a big fuss over my story. Writing about this magical place was quite easy for me, since I often visited there in my dreams and I knew communicating through thoughts was possible because I used to do it with my favorite toy, Lea. To me, everything that I wrote about seemed very typical and normal and I could not understand why my teacher and mother thought it to be so extraordinary.

CHAPTER 6

The Isis Connection

Every child has a superhero, singer, or television personality that they idolize. In the mid-1970s I became enthralled with the television series "The Secrets of Isis". The main character of this television series was a schoolteacher who finds an ancient mystical amulet that transforms her into a goddess/super-hero when she recites a specific incantation. The special amulet also gave her the power to fly with the assistance of strong swirling winds that would lift her to the sky. It is no surprise that I resonated with Isis having been experiencing frequent and vivid flying dreams for years before the show even aired on television. In my flying dreams, I would wait for a windy storm to lift me up to the sky taking me to places all over the world as we know it as well as to strange places or realms that existed somewhere else in the Universe. At that youthful age I dreamed of becoming like Isis and having superpowers that would enable me to fly while I was awake.

As the flying dreams continued, they became very real to me, so much so that there came a point where I believed that given the right set of circumstances, I could fly. Convinced that all I needed was an adequate runway and a strong gusty wind to help lift me into the air and soar high in the sky, it is with great embarrassment that I admit to testing this theory with the help of my best friend and sidekick, Danielle. The flying test was something we had to plan for because we needed a windy day.

After a couple of weeks of patiently waiting, that day finally came on a cold and windy day in November. I remember walking outside early Saturday morning and feeling the chilly wind chap my face as I watched the leaves from the maple trees in my front yard scatter all over the place. A feeling of dread came over me knowing my father would soon have me rake all the leaves into big piles and bag them up, but my attitude quickly brightened up because the weather was perfect for flying! Excited, I ran next door and knocked on Danielle's front door to alert her that the day we had been waiting for was finally here. I urged her to hurry up and get ready to come outside and join me before the wind settled down as I did not want to miss our chance.

I remember standing in the middle of the street in front of my house full of hope and excitement. My devoted helper, Danielle, had instructions to give me the go signal and then I would take off running as fast as I could down the street, leap into the air and hope the gusty winds would assist by lifting me to the sky! I was a chunky child so you can imagine my speed and agility left much to be desired. My first attempt at flying failed miserably as I leaped into the air only to fall quickly to the pavement like a lead balloon, scraping up my knees and elbows. Danielle looked on nervously chewing on her cuticles as I slowly peeled myself off the road. I gave her my assurance that I was fine and able to try again. However, I decided my take off technique needed improvement and incorporated twirling around three times before I began to run. To my dismay, this did not work either, it only made me dizzy resulting in falling to the ground faster. Danielle stood loyally in my driveway, but I was not sure if she was looking on in horror or admiration as I belly-flopped onto the pavement again. I was just as stubborn as I was imaginative, and wanted to try again, convinced the third attempt would be the charm. For my final attempt to fly, I incorporated reciting the same chant that my Isis idol from the television series chanted before taking off. There I stood in the middle of the street, gazing up to the heavens and shouting "O zephyr winds which blow on high, lift me now so I can fly" then I took off running, leaped into the air and just like the two previous attempts, fell flat on the street leaving me severely bruised and scraped with road gravel imbedded in me from head to toe. It is a miracle that I did not break any bones or worse. Admittedly, this was the most idiotic thing I have ever done in my life. Thinking about this event from my childhood always makes me cringe and laugh simultaneously. I wish we had iPhones back then, because the recording certainly would have made an award-winning hilarious video.

So, you may be asking yourself why I chose to share this incredibly embarrassing story of my Isis infatuation along with the silly notion that I could fly which resulted in subjecting myself to unnecessary pain and humiliation. I will tell you that when my Spirit Team inspired me to author this book, they indicated that I would begin to recall memories from my past and discover meanings to them as I wrote. As I drafted this very chapter, my soul guided me to further research the Egyptian Goddess Isis because apart from the television series that I watched as a child, I had no other knowledge about her. What I discovered is truly revealing.

According to ancient Egyptian mythology, Isis is one of the most important goddesses. Isis's role in the Afterlife was to restore the souls of deceased humans to wholeness like she did for her husband Osiris, King of Egypt, who was murdered by his jealous brother. She is the mother of Horus, the god of the Sky and Sun. Isis is portrayed as a healer and communicator and embodies the concepts of death and rebirth, symbolizing the transformative power of death and offering solace and guidance to the grieving.

The fact that I was drawn to the character and idea of Isis at an early age and then later developed into a psychic medium working with departed souls, the Afterlife and providing solace for the bereaved, is a remarkable parallel, but I would soon discover that there was more to my connection to Isis.

Shortly after working on this chapter and researching the Egyptian Goddess Isis, I attended a Forever Family Foundation Grief Retreat in Chester, Connecticut, as one of the guest mediums. There I had the pleasure of meeting another certified medium colleague, Dave Campbell. Dave is not only a psychic medium, but he is an amazing astrologer as well. In between our group mediumship sessions, we had time to get to know one another and during one of our conversations, I mentioned that I had begun to work on my book. I shared with Dave, that since I started writing, Spirit began showing me how things from my past and present are now connecting in my life. I specifically cited the infatuation that I had with the Isis television character when I was a child and how upon researching Isis, I discovered the connection to the Afterlife and working with souls. Right away Dave became intrigued and volunteered to do my astrological chart for me. I never had my astrological chart done before, so I was excited to learn what it would reveal. The amount of information that you can get from an astrological reading by providing your date and time of birth is impressive. According to Dave, this is what my astrological chart revealed:

"You have asteroid Isis at twenty degrees Virgo in your chart, conjunction to your chart ruler, Pluto. This gives you an affinity for Isis and all the themes that come with Isis, Egypt, Healing, and Magic. You also have Nephthys, Egyptian Goddess of the dead (connection to mediumship) sister of Isis, which is also in conjunction with your other chart ruler Mars."

My astrological chart information validates that my story had been written in the stars and imbedded in my soul the instant I was born. Even though my soul recognized this connection at an early age, it was not until I was much older that I was able to put the pieces of the puzzle of my life together and discover my soul's true destiny as a psychic medium. My Spirit Team's message became validated, and I was discovering and beginning to understand who I really was on a soul level.

CHAPTER 7

Near-Death Experience #1
My Life Review

So far I have had three significant and different encounters with the Afterlife known as near-death experiences (NDEs). Interestingly, all three of these occurrences were precipitated by adverse effects to medications. I have also come to understand that each near-death experience was an attempt by my soul to get me to realize my true destiny and bring me closer to my spiritual awareness and intuitive abilities. Looking back now, I realize that these NDEs were a big deal but at the time that they each occurred I was in The Confused Soulitude and did not recognize the signs from my soul. I also did not have any frame of reference, education, or any other exposure to near-death experiences to make me want to explore these glimpses of the Afterlife further in an effort to understand what really happened to me.

My first near-death experience occurred in the summer of 1986. I was working as an administrative training program coordinator in the city of White Plains, New York. One day my manager, Alex, came by my desk and dropped off participant training certificates that needed to get typed up for an upcoming training class. "By any chance could you have those ready for me by the end of the day?" he asked politely. I was busy assembling training manuals and when I looked up at him to reply, he exclaimed "Wow, you really got some sun this weekend!" I acknowledged his remark to be true as I had been outside that weekend, enjoying the summer sun by the pool. I let Alex know that I would have the certificates ready for him by noon. Minutes later, one of my co-workers, Lori, who was passing by my desk on her way back from grabbing a cup of coffee from the break room exclaimed "Somebody got some sun!"

I continued assembling the training manuals and after about fifteen minutes, I went into the breakroom to get myself a cup of coffee. When I entered the room, my co-workers already there exclaimed various comments in unison about how red or sunburnt I looked. This barrage of comments about my suntan seemed very odd so I immediately made my way down the hall to the restroom to have a look in the mirror. "Holy Moly!" I gasped when I saw my reflection in the mirror revealed a beet red face and neck. I lifted my shirt to see red blotches all over my torso area and began to panic. Suddenly it became difficult to breathe and I started feeling very light-headed. Thankfully, Alice, who was one of the co-workers that saw me in the breakroom, had followed me into the restroom concerned for my welfare. She found me sitting on the floor gasping for air. Alice ran back to the breakroom and yelled for someone to call an ambulance and then came back to sit with me on the restroom floor while we waited for medical assistance to arrive.

I could feel my throat beginning to close as my breathing became labored and it wasn't long before the paramedics arrived, loaded me onto a stretcher and into an ambulance. I was fading in and out and recalled my body was shaking and convulsing on the stretcher. I felt the sting of a needle injected into my thigh. Next, I remember seeing medical personnel standing around the stretcher shouting orders and I could hear loud beeping noises and then everything became fuzzy. Suddenly my body felt much lighter, and I realized that I was sitting with my legs crossed in front of me in an empty space with no floors or walls surrounded by bright light. The light was so intense that I lifted my hand to shield my eyes from it and then I perceived someone walking towards me. The overpowering light prohibited me from seeing any details of who this was, and I could only make out an outline of an illuminated figure. The illuminated figure placed an over-sized book on my lap. I noticed that the book had a worn, brown leather cover and appeared to be about two feet high and three feet wide in size. The pages of the enormous book illuminated a radiant soft golden glow that projected outward and upward into the empty space I was sitting in. As I looked down at the book, the pages started flipping forward on their own, revealing imagery of people, places, and events in my lifetime beginning from my birth to that present day. As the illuminated pages flipped in front of me, I remembered the people and experiences as well as the associated feelings and emotions connected to them.

When I regained consciousness, I found myself in a recovery room at the hospital and learned that I had suffered anaphylaxis due to an allergic reaction to an antibiotic that I had been taking. The next day, I was cleared to be discharged from the hospital and went home. I told my mother about the "strange dream" I had experienced in the hospital describing the detailed images that I saw in the huge, illuminated book from the first couple of years of my life. My mother was surprised that I could recall memories that occurred while I was still an infant and validated that the imagery was accurate. This was my first visit to the Other Side and having no prior knowledge about Afterlife experiences, I did not realize at the time that I had encountered a near-death experience in the form of a Life Review.

A couple of weeks after this NDE, something strange started happening when I was sleeping...I began experiencing sleep paralysis. During sleep paralysis, which usually occurs when a person is transitioning between the states of wakefulness and sleep, the person feels as if they are conscious, but they are unable to speak or move for seconds or even minutes. I was experiencing these episodes two to three times a month and they continued for months before they completely stopped. The sleep paralysis episodes were all similar in nature in that I would sense a presence as I lay flat on my back with my eyes wide open, conscious, but in a complete state of full-body paralysis. Then suddenly I would see myself come out of my body in spirit form, straddling my physical body and trying to pull on my arms to get me to sit up. The sleep paralysis prevented me from being able to sit up, and my head would be filled with a white noise humming/buzzing sound or vibration. Amidst the white noise, I would hear in my mind a voice repeatedly saying, "You need to raise yourself up, you need to raise yourself up." I was baffled as to why I kept hearing these same words repeated in every sleep paralysis occurrence. "You need to raise yourself up" was stating the obvious to me as I was not able to physically move during these occurrences.

For years, I wondered why I would hear such a strange message but now, with my knowledge and ability of spirit communication, I have come to understand that my soul was encouraging me to raise myself up spiritually, in other words, raise my vibration to become a medium and connect with the Other Side. My soul was literally trying to tell me what my destiny was and how to do it but again, having no frame of reference to the metaphysical world, I did not understand the message and so it was ignored. I was still in The Confused Soulitude.

The Universe is persistent in leading you to your soul's true destiny and so another attempt to get it through my thick head occurred a couple of years later in the form of a second near-death experience. This one would prove to be a little more medically aggressive and finally instill a curiosity in me to explore the metaphysical world.

CHAPTER 8

Near-Death Experience #2 Through the Tunnel and into the Glow

It was a cool March morning in 1990 and my day started like any other workday for the past two years. I was standing on the platform of the New Hamburg, New York, train station waiting for the Metro-North 6:15 AM train destined for New York City. I hated waiting on that platform in the morning when it was still dark, especially when I had to deal with the humidity, rain, or sleet and snow in the winter months as the platform offered no covered areas to seek shelter under at that time. My daily train commute took two hours each way. That was four hours of my life every day spent commuting on the train, leaving for New York City when it was still dark and arriving back home after 8:00 PM when it was dark again. It was miserable and looking back, I do not know how I did it for so long.

That particular morning, I was feeling a bit under the weather with a sinus infection and seasonal allergies and feeling bad made the commute a hundred times worse. I had been taking prescribed antibiotics and an antihistamine for days now and I was praying that they would kick in soon and provide some relief. When I arrived at Grand Central Station, I proceeded as usual with grabbing a bagel and a cup of coffee from a street vendor and then began walking to my work location in midtown Manhattan. I had followed in my mother's footsteps and had been working as an administrative assistant since graduating high school and just started a new job at a commercial real estate company. Realizing I was moving a little sluggishly, I quickened my pace to avoid being late. After walking a couple of blocks, I began sweating and took off my jacket and tied it around my waist, wondering why I was feeling so hot and clammy when it was a cool brisk morning. As I got closer to the office, I noticed that my breathing became labored. I assumed it was just the allergy medicine and my sinus congestion making me feel wonky and trudged on. By the time I arrived at the office, I was short of breath and sweating profusely. My hair was sticking to my forehead like a cat had just licked it and my blouse was damp and clinging to me. I grabbed a cup of water from the water cooler, sat down at my desk and proceeded to blot my face with napkins from the paper bag containing my bagel to try and absorb the sweat and cool off. Maria, the other secretary that sat next to me, had also just walked in, and started swapping out the sneakers she arrived in for the black pumps she kept under her desk. "Good Morning" she said cheerfully as she bent down to put on her shoes and then when she looked up at me, she exclaimed "Are you alright? You look extremely pale, and you do not look well!"

I was far from being all right at that point. I was sweating, shaking, and panting because my heart was beating so fast it was taking my breath away. "I think I'm going to pass out," I mumbled weakly. Maria shouted out for our manager, Mr. Sinclair, who came running quickly. "I think she needs to go to the hospital" Maria stated. Mr. Sinclair gave me a quick concerned glance, nodded, and instructed Maria to call for his personal car service to come around the front of the building. He knew it was morning rush hour traffic and his personal driver had a better chance of getting me to the hospital quickly rather than an ambulance having to fight through New York City traffic to get to me and then transport me to the hospital. That smart decision was instrumental in saving my life. Next, Maria and Mr. Sinclair hurriedly rolled me down the hallway in the office chair that I was still sitting in and into the elevator and then transferred me into the back of the town car that was waiting in front of the office building to transport me to the hospital. Mr. Sinclair instructed the driver to get me to the nearest hospital as soon as possible and told Maria to go with me and keep him apprised of my condition.

All during that ride in the back of the town car I remember thinking that things were escalating quickly to a critical situation, and I was fearful of dying. My heart was beating incredibly hard and fast, and it felt as if it would leap out of my chest. Somehow, I had the mental and physical capacity to reach into my pocketbook still strapped across my body, grab a pen, and scribble six words along with my parents' phone number on one of the napkins I was still holding. I handed it to Maria and watched as her face went white as she read the six foreboding words that I had written on the napkin "tell my parents I love them." She yelled out to the driver "Go faster!!" I felt the lurch of the town car as the driver hit the gas and did his best to maneuver through mid-town Manhattan morning rush hour traffic. He was cursing non-stop now and laying on his horn trying to clear a path to the hospital. It seemed like forever, but we finally arrived at the hospital. Maria leaped out of the car and ran into the emergency room and within seconds, she ran back with emergency room staff behind her. They quickly hoisted me onto a stretcher and wheeled me into a room full of clinicians and medical equipment.

A whirlwind of events ensued as clinicians were shouting orders while others were putting wires on my chest, taking my blood pressure, sticking an IV in my arm, and drawing blood. I remember feeling cold, light-headed, and thinking surely these people can hear my heart beating without any instruments because it felt like I could hear it pounding loudly in my own ears along with this strange white noise vibration sound.

Suddenly, I found myself floating right below the ceiling. I was looking down at my body on the hospital bed watching the emergency room clinicians flutter around me. I saw the doctor grab two defibrillator paddles and place them on my chest, shocking my body and causing it to jolt off the table like a rag doll. Next, I was aware that I was no longer floating near the ceiling but instead, inside a small tunnel. I would describe the tunnel and the way that I moved through it like being in a closed MRI machine that travelled through space. This may sound strange, but it seemed as if I was moving slow but fast at the same time, like the feeling you have when experiencing a virtual high-speed simulated amusement park ride at Disney World. I was lying on my back moving feet first through the tunnel and toward an incredibly bright light. As I drew nearer to that light, I felt the atmosphere change around me. It felt electrically charged and that strange white noise vibration filled my being. The light was so bright, like looking directly into the sun but with more intensity and no heat. Oddly enough, I was not afraid and instead felt a sense of eagerness to get closer to the source of the light. Finally, I arrived at the end of the tunnel and became overwhelmed with feelings of love and jubilation as the soles of my feet sank into "the glow" as if it were made of Jello. I became immersed in that beautiful glow and that strange white noise vibration intensified, seeming to come from within and outside of me at the same time. That is all I remember.

I woke up the next day in a hospital room confused and wondering why my wrists were wrapped in bandages. The nurse attending to me explained the bandages were from testing for arterial blood gases. My doctor arrived minutes later and informed me that I had endured a V-tach (Ventricular Tachycardia) episode and was incredibly fortunate as my situation could have been fatal had I not made it to the hospital in time. After further testing and observation, the doctor could still not provide any medical explanation for what caused the V-tach, and so I was cleared to go home and instructed to rest for a couple of weeks before returning to work and my normal routine.

I would discover years later in a news article that randomly came to my attention, that my V-tach incident was caused by the combination of the antihistamine and antibiotic that I had been taking at the time. In the later 1990's the Food and Drug Administration (FDA) took that antihistamine off the market due to the discovery of it causing fatal heart rhythm issues and other adverse interactions when taken simultaneously with other medications like the one I had been prescribed.

I was in my early twenties at this time and still ignorant about experiences with the Afterlife, so I did not make a big deal out of this event, which unbeknownst to me, turned out to be my second near-death experience. I went back to work in New York City and to my usual routine, or so I thought. My encounter with the Other Side triggered my extrasensory gifts that had been mostly dormant since I was a child. This sparked my soul's curiosity and desire to learn more about the metaphysical world and soon I would be pulled in that direction.

CHAPTER 9

The Metaphysical Pull

Something changed in me after my second-near-death experience. Somehow my extrasensory abilities intensified. Occasionally, I had experienced seeing flashes of images associated with strangers ever since my first near-death experience, but now this was happening more frequently. It would often occur while sitting next to someone on the subway or train. I was beginning to think something was different about me.

One day, a couple of months after my second near-death experience, I left my office to grab lunch at one of my usual places but subconsciously began walking in a different direction. Normally, on my lunch break, I would pick up soup, salad, or a sandwich from one of the nearby delicatessens within a three-block radius from my office in Midtown Manhattan. I am not sure what made me walk in a different direction on that day or what I was looking for, but suddenly a big blinking sign in an old brownstone window that read "Psychic Readers" appeared before me and I felt drawn to go in.

I walked up to the front desk and asked the gentlemen receptionist to explain what a psychic reading entailed. He explained that the psychics could provide answers to questions about life and predict my future. The explanation intrigued me, so I purchased a fifteen-minute reading and was handed a ticket with the number twenty-six on it and instructed to sit on the entryway bench to wait for my number to be called out. I waited nervously for about ten minutes not knowing what to expect.

Finally, I heard my ticket number called out and a tall, pale, thin woman with short, platinum blonde hair and eyes heavily accentuated with dark liner, approached me. I remember thinking she looked very much like David Bowie. "Hello, I'm Jane, follow me," she said, and I followed her to a small booth upholstered in dark red vinyl material at the back of the room. Jane asked me to pick a tarot card deck from the vast collection she had stored in a glittery gold box on the table. I picked the tarot deck closest to me and per Jane's instruction began to shuffle them to put my energy into the cards. I shuffled, gave the deck back to Jane and she began putting the cards down one by one on the table as she relayed information about my life and future events. I was totally fascinated how Jane knew things from the different cards that she flipped over even though everything she said was quite generic and could relate to just about anyone. Nevertheless, something about this reading stirred up something deep inside of me and I continued to have readings with Jane and other psychic readers for months afterwards.

Watching and listening during tarot card readings made me think it was pretty straight forward as every card had a designated meaning, so in 1991 I purchased my first tarot card deck. I remember thinking to myself, how hard could it be to flip the card over and say what it means? I was always a quick learner and having that keen sense of just knowing things, or claircognizance, I assumed reading tarot cards would be quite easy. Also, since I was seeing images associated with strangers more frequently, I was curious to understand why. I hoped that working with the tarot cards might uncover any potentially hidden intuitive abilities that I might possess.

After I got home from work that evening, I took out the little instructional pamphlet that came with the tarot cards and began to read the card descriptions and meanings and tried to commit them to memory. I was confident that I could memorize the meanings easily and be able to understand how to read the cards, but this proved to be much more difficult than I anticipated. I read those tarot card descriptions again and again, but they did not resonate with me or stick in my head, leaving me baffled and frustrated.

Now, I am a Gemini, and true to my astrological sign, if something does not attract or hold my attention right away, I cast it aside and that became the fate of those tarot cards. Even though I was frustrated in not being able to make an immediate connection to them, I could not bring myself to throw them away and instead, decided to put them inside a small storage chest for miscellaneous items that I kept in my bedroom closet.

At this point in my life, I was still in The Confused Soulitude, but I was beginning to feel a pull towards the metaphysical and spiritual world. I thought that I was ready to explore and learn about any heightened perceptive abilities I might possess, but the Universe threw me a curve ball and shortly after I purchased that tarot card deck negative influences started dominating my life, shifting me to The Closed Soulitude. That deck of tarot cards would remain in the storage chest in my bedroom closet for the next ten years, as I experienced the most challenging times of my life caught between The Confused and The Closed Soulitudes.

At the time, I did not understand the purpose for those ten long years of feeling lost, helpless, and hopeless, but there were much needed lessons of self-love and self-worth that I had to experience to evolve spiritually. I needed to gain the courage and strength to take measures to break out of The Closed Soulitude and begin relying on my faith and trust in Spirit and the Universe to assist in removing the negative obstacles that were preventing me from discovering my soul's true destiny.

CHAPTER 10

Flying and Floating

There are different philosophies and opinions about flying dreams. My opinion is that these dreams represent your soul's freedom, revealing any unconscious abilities or hidden talents that you may possess that can elevate you to a new level of understanding, intuition, or higher consciousness. Native Americans, Tibetans and Hindus share a belief that flying in your dreams represents departed souls and your ability to establish emotional connections with those spirits. Flying dreams are also associated with the phenomenon known as astral projection where the dreamer experiences higher spiritual vibrations allowing them to fly alone with confidence.

Many people have flying dreams, and they are all different and unique. As a young child my flying dreams would consist of visiting magical lands that were bright and beautiful where I would sing, dance, and play with other children and animals. Everyone I encountered in these magical places understood each other without having to talk. When I was in middle school, my flying dreams changed in that they usually began with me searching for a wide-open space that could serve as a runway for me to run and gain speed before jumping and soaring into the sky. The other aspect of these dreams that was significant for me is that I always felt a sense of apprehension when flying over a wide-open space, crater, or big body of water, fearful of not having enough energy to make it over them successfully to a safe landing. Often in these dreams, I came remarkably close to just barely clearing those spaces before losing energy and when this happened, I would feel a surge of pride and confidence in my accomplishment.

Frequently my dreams started out waiting for a good gusty wind and then I would start running across the roof of a very tall building, convincing myself to summon up the courage and confidence to jump off, trusting that I can fly away safely and not plunge to my death. These flying dreams were always testing me and trying to get me to overcome my own self-doubt which I realize now has been a common theme throughout my life. This particular flying dream came often and remained consistently the same for years until my second near-death experience occurred in my early twenties.

After my second near-death experience, my flying dreams changed and intensified and I was able to sustain my energy longer, allowing me to fly higher and farther into the Universe. Also, the starting point of my dreams changed, and lightning became a prevalent factor versus the wind. For the longest time in my flying dreams, like my childhood idol, Isis, it was the wind that assisted in lifting me up, but I now have come to understand that the wind represents my consciousness and my ability to raise my consciousness or vibration. The lightning, I have come to understand, is a metaphor for the electrically charged atmosphere or electromagnetic energy needed for the brain to reach higher levels of consciousness. This deduction coincides with the fact that the stronger the winds and lightning are in my dreams, the higher and further I can fly into the Universe.

With the changes cited above, my new repetitive flying dream that began after my second near-death experience starts out with me standing in front of a large glowing cross stationed on top of an old church steeple. The white glow of the cross that stands about fifteen feet tall illuminates the atmosphere around me. I am always barefoot and wearing a plain white nightgown that falls just below my knees. From where I am standing, I can see the tips of the trees and mountains in the distance for miles and miles on all sides of me. The heavens are heavily decorated with millions of twinkling stars. The wind starts to pick up and I can feel the light mist of rain on my face, which is warm and soothing. I knowingly plant my feet firmly on the roof to brace myself for the storm and gale force winds that are about to come. I can sense the electricity in the air even before I see and hear the lightning crackling around me lighting up the sky like a fireworks show on the fourth of July. I know I need to be patient and wait for the electric energy to build. My mind, body and spirit feel so connected and blended with the energetic atmosphere that it is hard for me to decipher if I am the source of the light emanating from the cross behind me and the lightning in the sky or are they both somehow generating me?

I stand ready with my arms extended down on my sides and look up into the starry night. Then, the moment I have been waiting for finally arrives where the energy pinnacles and I lift off the rooftop and soar high into the heavens and beyond for another adventure. Despite the chaotic weather system that I find myself immersed in, I feel warm and safe in this environment and flying through the storm leaves me exhilarated. To this day, I continue to have this same recurring dream. I do not think it is by coincidence that I ended up moving from New York to the Tampa Bay area of Florida that is often referred to as the "Lightning Capital of North America" and is no stranger to severe thunderstorms, tornadoes, and hurricanes.

Once I started providing mediumship readings, I began having floating dreams in addition to the recurring flying dream. My floating dreams are quite different from my flying dreams. The flying dreams take me to places high in the sky, all over the world and into the universe and conversely, my floating dreams take place in everyday life scenarios and buildings. The floating dream locations vary from office buildings, to schools, wedding venues, public streets, and other populated areas.

Another notable difference is that during most of my flying dreams I experience different destinations as a silent observer taking in my surroundings and typically do not encounter or see any people. However, in my floating dreams, I am always in a public venue surrounded by and interacting with lots of people who are onlookers to my ability to float. The way I float also varies in the dreams as sometimes I lay flat on my stomach and hover inches from a ceiling, gliding through hallways or rooms. If I am standing vertically, I can move around as if I am levitating about a foot off the ground. Frequently, I sit with my legs crossed in front of me and zip around, weaving in and out of crowds of people as if I were riding an invisible magic carpet. In these floating dreams, I enjoy interacting with various people by doing tricks for them like somersaults, floating over water, or floating upside down. I shout out to the onlookers trying to get their attention by asking them to watch my tricks.

There are several opinions about the meaning of floating in dreams, but to me these dreams signify my spiritual growth and control and trust over my own psychic energy and abilities. I believe that in these floating dreams; my soul is encouraging me to reach out to people and assist them in raising their vibration and instill a belief in a higher level of consciousness and healing through spirit communication.

CHAPTER 11

Robert,
An Angel Among Us

I am a firm believer that angels, soul helpers, guides, or whatever label you would like to give them walk among us every day. These special individuals may come into our lives for just a few seconds, a brief period of time, or they may stay with us for the duration of our lifetime with the purpose of guiding our souls towards growth, healing, and alignment. Sometimes they appear out of nowhere but seem to arrive at that point in your life when you are at the crossroads, struggling or in desperate need of a helping hand to lift you up or out of your circumstances. They are the friendly faces bringing words of encouragement and hope. They are the mentors and guides that steer us towards our path of enlightenment. I was fortunate to meet one of these special helpers who was watching out for me and lifted me up when I needed a helping hand.

About eight years into my first marriage, I became extremely ill. I was experiencing terrible stomach and shoulder pain and was having difficulty eating certain foods. After a few visits to the emergency room, seeing a doctor and reviewing bloodwork results, I received a vague diagnosis of pancreatitis for which a very bland diet was suggested to calm the symptoms. I followed my doctor's guidance, but the bland diet was not helping to alleviate the symptoms and after more weeks of enduring pain, one morning it became unbearable, and I fell to the floor in agony. I yelled out for my oldest son, Nicholas, who was almost five years old at the time, to bring the cordless telephone to me so I could call my parents, who now lived in the same neighborhood, to come and watch my boys while I went to the hospital. My parents arrived within minutes and the ambulance followed shortly after to take me to the hospital where I was admitted and began to undergo more testing.

By the second day, left with nothing to do but lie in the bed waiting for doctors and test results, I began to get very worried. I was sure there was something more wrong with me than the original pancreatitis diagnosis. I started to think the worst and became consumed with fear and panic thinking the doctors would come back with a terrible or life-threatening diagnosis. I was so worried about my children wondering what would become of them if something should happen to me. I had been in a relationship for years that affected my happiness and self-esteem. I did not know who I was or what my purpose was anymore, other than being a good mother to my two wonderful boys. They were the only reason I continued on, resigned that I had made poor life decisions and had to deal with the consequences. That morning as I lie in the hospital bed awaiting news, I began to pray beseeching God to let me be healthy so I could raise my children. In return, I promised to eliminate the negative aspects of my life and make the changes necessary to raise myself up and be strong for the betterment of my boys. That afternoon, a Gastroenterologist visited me. I previously had an MRI done of my gallbladder from one of the prior emergency room visits which came back normal, but the physician stated he wanted to do another test called a HIDA scan which is an imaging procedure using a radioactive tracer that shows how well your liver, bile ducts and gallbladder are functioning. That afternoon they performed the test, and later that evening the physician returned to give me the results. The

HIDA scan revealed that my gallbladder was diseased and not functioning properly and they would be removing it the next day. I let out a huge sigh of relief to finally have a real diagnosis with a solution that involved removing an organ that I could comfortably live without. I immediately called my parents to share the good news and told them to tell my boys that I would be home in a couple of days. Feeling immensely grateful, I silently thanked God profusely for answering my prayers and within days of returning home from the hospital, I made good on my end of the bargain and phoned a divorce attorney to set up a consultation. I had spent the last eight years of my life in the Closed Soulitude as a victim of my negative circumstances and this was the first step I would take to regain control of my life and move in a more positive direction.

This was an exceedingly tough time for me as I navigated through challenging divorce proceedings while working a full-time job and having full-time responsibility for my two small children. In the summertime when nursery school/kindergarten was out, I would enroll Nicholas and Anthony in the onsite summer daycare program offered at my place of employment. The boys especially looked forward to eating breakfast in the corporate cafeteria before I dropped them off at the daycare center where they enjoyed playing with the other children.

It was during the summer of 2001, when I first met Robert. He seemed to appear out of nowhere one day as I was standing on the breakfast line with my boys in the cafeteria. He was a thin, African American man who looked to be in his fifties. Robert was wearing all white; a white shirt rolled up at the sleeves along with white pants under a white overall apron. I could not tell if he had hair because he was wearing the white cafeteria staff cap that fit snugly on his head. He was busy cleaning off the countertop next to me with a damp rag and then cheerfully looked my way and greeted me in a soft but gravelly voice that had a bit of southern drawl "Good Morning Miss Connie," he said smiling and flashing pearly white teeth. I noticed the name plate pinned on the front of his apron indicated his name was "Robert," so I greeted him back using his name. Then he tousled the hair on each of my boys' heads and said, "Listen to your mother. She knows what's best for you." Robert then gave me a nod and a smile, told us to have a blessed day and then grabbed a nearby bucket and mop and proceeded to clean the floors. I grabbed our breakfast trays and proceeded to the cafeteria dining area wondering how Robert knew my name, but then assumed he must have seen my ID badge hanging from my belt, just like I noticed his name tag on his uniform.

The next morning, the boys and I saw Robert again and he cheerfully wished us a good morning and then told Nicholas and Anthony that they were lucky to have such a wonderful mother who took such loving care of them. I continued to see Robert in the mornings for several weeks. He would find me either at the coffee bar or breakfast line and always offered a pleasant greeting followed by some kind and uplifting words like "smile, it's going to be a great day", "good things are around the corner", "I know you are good person, and good things happen to good people, just have faith". Robert was just an all-around nice guy, and these kind words and brief morning encounters lifted my spirits during this tough time for me, so much so, that I began to look forward to my morning cup of coffee and cup of cheerfulness from Robert. Then suddenly one day he was gone. I looked for him for the next few days and when he did not appear, I began asking the cafeteria workers if they knew what had happened to Robert. No one knew who I was referring to, which I found very strange. Time went by and I forgot about Robert, my divorce became finalized, and I started moving on with my life.

A couple of years later, while at home watching television one evening, I started having difficulty breathing which I later found out was due to an allergic reaction to the dye in M&Ms candy that I had been eating. I called an ambulance and then telephoned my parents to come and watch the boys. At the hospital I received medication to keep my airways open, and having had allergic reactions before, I knew I just needed to rest and give the medication time to work. While I lay there resting in the hospital room, someone knocked on the door. I called out for them to enter and then stared in disbelief and confusion as I witnessed Robert from the cafeteria appear in my room, looking exactly as I remembered him. "Robert?!" I exclaimed in confusion, "What are you doing here?" He smiled that kind smile flashing his pearly white teeth and then spoke to me in that familiar gravelly voice and said "Hello Miss Connie, I am just checking to make sure that you are all right. I can see that you are good, so I will be on my way," and with that he waved goodbye, turned, and walked out of the room. I never saw Robert again.

For the life of me, I could not understand how Robert found me years later in the hospital which was located in a different city from where I worked. This was absolutely bizarre! My parents came to pick me up from the hospital and I told them about my encounter with Robert. At the risk of sounding insane, I told them that I thought Robert was some kind of angel looking out for me. What other explanation could there be? Then, my mother shared something remarkably interesting with me. She told me that she had a miscarriage before I was born. The baby was a boy and they had named him Robert.

In the last few years, Robert, my deceased brother, has come through during readings with other mediums, saying that he is watching over me like a guardian angel and I know this to be true as I frequently feel his loving presence around me.

CHAPTER 12

My First Premonition
Touched by an Angel

It was February 2003, and we had just finished dinner and my children were jumping up and down with excitement upon receiving the news that we were going to the Florida State Fair on the weekend. Anthony was about to turn four years old, and Nicholas was almost seven and I thought they were at a good age to enjoy and experience their first fair. The boys decided to engage in a game of hide and seek while I cleaned up after dinner. It was amusing to watch them play because Anthony was usually hiding somewhere in plain sight, making him a quick find, but being a good big brother, Nicholas would always pretend that he didn't see Anthony right away to make the game fun.

After the boys had been playing the game for a while, I heard Nicholas frantically calling out for Anthony. He was running in and out of the bedrooms, bathrooms and living room and then came into the kitchen. "Mommy, I can't find Anthony!" he exclaimed. This was very strange because Anthony was usually very easily found in one of three of his known hiding places. "Did you check your closet?" I inquired and Nicholas nodded his head indicating yes. "Did you look behind the couch?" He nodded yes again. "Did you look under my bed?" Another affirmative nod. Nicholas was baffled and exclaimed "I looked everywhere, and I cannot find Anthony and he is not answering when I call him!"

I put the last dish away and headed towards the living room to join the game and assist in the search for Anthony, but as I took a couple of steps forward, I suddenly felt this horrible sense of fear and loss. The enormous emotion of panic that followed was so intense that it made me nauseous, and I clutched my stomach and fell to my knees on the living room floor. I started screaming like a crazy person "Anthony! Anthony! Where are you?" Nicholas looked terrified as he stared at me screaming on the living floor. I felt like I could not catch my breath and then suddenly my little boy came running out from the bathroom down the hall. "Here I am Mommy!" Anthony shouted. I grabbed him in my arms, hugging him fiercely and sobbing hysterically. "I was in the bathtub!" Anthony proudly stated knowing he had found a clever hiding place and outsmarted us. And at that, I burst out laughing. I am sure my children thought their mother had gone nuts and I was leaning towards thinking that myself as I reflected on the series of events and my strange and drastic reaction to a harmless game of hide and seek. What was wrong with me?

Next thing you know, it is Saturday morning, and I am lathering up the boys with sunscreen and packing my tote bag with juice boxes, snacks, wipes, and extra clothes for our day at the Florida State Fair. It was a beautiful sunny day, and we spent the morning feeding goats and llamas in the petting zoo, riding on the carousel, runaway train and spinning cup ride and then walking through the fun house of mirrors. Of course, being Florida it was extremely hot outside and I was eager to take a break and sit down somewhere in the shade for lunch.

As we made our way through the exhibition halls, we came across the rock-climbing wall and watched children Nicholas's age and older try to climb to the top. Nicholas wanted to give it a try, so we made our way to the counter to sign up. "How long of a wait is it?" I inquired and the exhibit attendant replied, "about fifteen minutes." I wrote Nicholas's name down on the waiting list and went to grab Anthony's hand to go wait on the bench for our turn and that is when my world turned upside down.

During the few seconds of this interaction, my son, Anthony, went missing at the Florida State Fair! I looked around frantically and could not see him in the crowd. "Nicholas, where is your brother?" I demanded anxiously. He just shrugged his shoulders indicating he had no idea. And then, it was like déjà vu and that same feeling of fear, loss, and panic that I experienced previously when we could not find Anthony during the hide and seek game returned. I felt engulfed by a tidal wave of nausea, and I fell to my knees in the middle of the crowd and started screaming "Anthony, Anthony!" over and over. I was in a waking nightmare. My four-year-old child was missing at the Florida State Fair, lost among approximately 40,000 people. I wanted to die.

I got up, grabbed Nicholas's hand, and started pushing my way through the crowd, screaming Anthony's name. After about ten minutes, I spotted a police officer and sprinted towards him dragging Nicholas behind me. "Officer!" I yelled as I approached him, "Please help me!" I quickly gave him the details of Anthony's disappearance along with his physical description, attire, and my phone number. He immediately radioed for backup and within minutes more police officers arrived. A nice police officer took Nicholas back with her to wait at the fairgrounds police station, and we all dispersed in different directions to search for my son.

I do not know how I was even functioning as I ran desperately and wildly through the crowd screaming Anthony's name repeatedly. After what seemed like an eternity, but in reality was approximately twenty minutes, I felt someone grab my shoulder from behind me. I stopped and turned around to see who it was. There was no one there but I found myself looking in the direction of an elderly woman standing next to a toddler in a stroller. We locked gazes and I walked towards her and asked if she had seen Anthony, and she nodded her head indicating yes. The elderly woman explained that they encountered a little boy matching Anthony's description wandering around by himself and her daughter left about ten minutes ago to bring him to the police station. I thanked her profusely, wiping the tears from my face and ran like hell to the police station. I almost collapsed with relief as I entered the small building and saw Anthony sitting next to his older brother, Nicholas, smiling and sipping on a juice box. I ran towards him and squeezed him so hard he started yelling that I was hurting him. Thankfully, Anthony seemed unphased by the whole ordeal that just rocked my world and just wanted me to stop smothering him with hugs and kisses.

Later that evening, after I had put the boys to bed, I reflected on the tumultuous day that I had just endured. I remembered feeling the hand on my shoulder which made me stop, look, and glance in the direction of the old woman who had found my son. How strange, that in a crowd of thousands of people, that someone/something would make me stop and face the person who could lead me to Anthony. I felt certain that higher forces were at work here to help me find my son.

I also reflected on how I had felt the immense loss, sense of panic and fear of not being able to find Anthony during the hide and seek game prior to the fair, as if foretelling something to come. It was then that I realized I had experienced a warning premonition. I continue to have premonitions. Sometimes they are warnings, like seeing a snake before it appears in my path, and others are visions of predictive events that eventually come to fruition.

CHAPTER 13

Near-Death Experience #3 Meeting Jesus

It was Spring 2003, and I was recovering from a surgical procedure and still feeling the effects of the anesthesia and medication that I had been given. Suddenly, I found myself immersed in beautiful, fluffy, rolling white clouds and then as the clouds dissipated, I was standing in a very lush green field filled with multi-colored wildflowers. A group of young children were running towards me. As they came closer, I noticed their glowing jubilant faces and sparkling eyes and their joyful laughter filled the air. Everything and everyone looked intensified in vivid colors. Two of the children grabbed my hands and we all formed a circle and began to dance and sing, going round and round while looking up at the cerulean, blue sky and feeling the warmth of the golden rays of sunshine on our faces. I felt so carefree and happy singing and dancing with the children. We were singing a beautiful song, and I knew that it was not something that I had learned on the Earth plane, but somehow I knew the words and the language. Then the children began to slow down their dancing and began to move to each side of me while looking off into the distance.

As I followed their gaze; I saw a man approaching us. His hair was brown, parted in the middle and fell just below his shoulders. He had a mustache and beard that touched down right above a large wooden cross hanging from a thin piece of leather that adorned his chest. As the man came closer, I noticed he was wearing a simple white tunic and leather sandals. But it was his eyes that I will always remember. The man came close to me, gazed straight into my eyes, and asked, "Do you like it here?" His eyes were like looking into an ocean, they were ever changing with intense hues of blue, green, and then brown radiating flecks of gold. I remember the sensation of feeling like he was not looking at me or through me but looking at the whole of me and there was an understanding that he knew everything about me.

Being raised as a Catholic, and being in his presence, I believed this man to be Jesus. I answered his question fervently "Oh yes, I love it here!" but then I looked around and asked "but, where are my children?" Jesus laughed aloud and then smiled and replied, "It is not their time yet." I nodded in acknowledgment and began to sing and dance with the young children again. After a few more minutes they stopped and turned to look at Jesus who then posed the question to me again "Do you like it here?," and like before, I replied "Yes, I love it here...but where are my children?" Jesus looked at me and smiled and said, "It is not their time yet, and it is not yours either, for you have yet to become who you were meant to be."

I woke from this state of altered consciousness reflecting on what had just happened to me, not realizing I had my third near-death experience. I thought about the words that Jesus spoke to me and wondered, who am I supposed to be? The answer to this question became a little bit clearer to me a few weeks later.

CHAPTER 14

Reading Tarot Cards Came as a Shock to Me

Shortly after my third near-death experience, I received a random call from a woman named Louise, an event coordinator looking for a tarot card reader for a psychic fair in south Florida. Somehow, she got my name and number from a friend of a friend of a friend. Immediately I thought Louise must be desperate to reach out to me, and my assumption was confirmed when she shared that there were last-minute cancellations, and the psychic fair was in two days. As she relayed the details of the event a spark of interest grew within me. I asked Louise to wait on the phone for a minute while I ran to my bedroom closet and pulled out a storage chest to look for my deck of tarot cards placed there over ten years ago. I bought the deck in 1991 in New York City but became frustrated when I read the traditional meanings printed on the enclosed instructional booklet. I did not feel a connection to the cards, so I put them in the storage chest and never looked at them again until that moment. Thankfully, the tarot cards were still there, so I ran back to the phone and accepted the invitation to read at the psychic fair.

Before you know it, Saturday morning arrived and as I was getting myself ready to go to the psychic fair reality began to set in. What in the heck was I doing? I was going to a psychic fair to read tarot cards that I didn't even know the meanings of, not to mention that I had never given anyone a reading before! What was I thinking? I started to have a panic attack and began sweating and feeling nauseous. I sat down on my bed and tried to compose myself by taking deep breaths to calm down. I realized that I had acted hastily on a whim and should not have agreed to do the event. I knew Louise had cancellations and she needed help so I decided that I would still show up but tell her that I did not feel comfortable reading tarot cards and ask if I could assist in another way. I began to feel better with this approach and got in my car to drive to the event.

The event center where the psychic fair was being held was already crowded when I arrived. As soon as I walked through the door, Louise greeted me and motioned to quickly follow her to the far side of the building to a small room that had a little table and two chairs in it. Louise's face was red, and she seemed flustered. I felt a lump in my throat as I summoned the courage to tell her that I did not feel comfortable providing readings, but I managed to blurt it out. Louise was not pleased, and she did not allow me to back out of the commitment, adamantly telling me to sit at that table because she needed a body there. Then she attempted to make me feel better by saying that I may not have any customers because there were more psychics located in the front and middle of the building, and I was at the very far end. I reluctantly agreed to stay and sat in one of the chairs and started praying that no one would come my way.

I sat there sweating and fidgeting nervously for about twenty minutes and then a woman came through the door, sat down in the chair opposite to me and asked for a reading. She was an attractive woman with light brown hair who looked to be in her mid-fifties. I tried to make small talk with the woman by asking if this was her first tarot card reading experience, and her answer only elevated my level of anxiety as she shared that she visited psychics frequently. I grabbed my tarot cards and clumsily attempted to pull the cards out of the tight sleeve which proved to be difficult being a brand-new deck with the cards removed only once before. My fumbling did not go unnoticed as the woman visibly winced and I am sure she was thinking I was a fraud—and with good reason to.

I did not know what to do with the tarot cards, so I shuffled them a bit and then started putting them down randomly in a circle. I continued laying down the cards in the circular pattern and then decided the space in the middle looked bare, so I put three cards across in the middle. I repeated the circular pattern then three in the middle until I used all seventy-six cards. Now what? The woman looked perturbed and asked me if I was going to say anything. I began to sweat again and feel nauseous. I took a deep breath and stared down at the random messy piles of cards that lay before me and then something strange and incredible happened. I felt an electric shock come in through the top of my head and shoot through me, radiating down my arms and then through the rest of my body, leaving me with a tingling sensation all over. As I looked down at the cards, thoughts, images, and words came into my awareness. I began to talk.

I told the woman that I felt that there was a secret or some hidden information that recently became revealed, and it had something to do with a family member. I also saw a legal matter involving a lawyer and important documents. I saw that she would be taking a trip to a foreign country within the next two weeks to two months as well as a generous sum of money coming to this woman connected to someone who had died. I paused and asked the woman if any of this made any sense to her. The woman smiled and began to validate the information I had given her. First, the woman shared that she had recently found out that she had been adopted because of receiving communication from her biological father's attorney notifying her of his death. Her biological father had lived in France, and to her surprise, she was his sole heir and had inherited a sizable amount of money and a large home. The woman went on to tell me that she had a trip planned in a couple of weeks to France to settle that business. I was completely dumbfounded wondering how I could have known this information. I continued the reading, looking at the other piles of cards and provided additional information which the woman also validated. At the end of the reading, the woman profusely thanked me, expressing that it was one of the best readings she ever experienced.

I was confused, thrilled, overwhelmed, and terrified all at once. What had just happened? How did I look at the random pictures on the small piles of tarot cards that I had made and know specific information? What was that weird shock that ran through me? It was all too much for me to grasp and no longer able to contain all the emotions I had been dealing with, I ran quickly for the bathroom and threw up. Yes, that is how I started reading tarot cards…I was literally shocked into doing it!

I continued to read tarot cards in that same manner and format for friends and once I had my process down, eventually for clients. I found that I would receive information from Spirit from the various images on the tarot cards and how they were grouped together. Now I finally understood why I could not connect with the tarot cards over ten years ago when I first bought them; I was never meant to read tarot the traditional way. I was meant to use the cards as a tool to connect with my Spirit Team. To this day, I continue to provide psychic tarot card readings in the same manner, using the original deck of tarot cards that I bought in 1991. I still cannot tell you the traditional meanings of the tarot cards.

CHAPTER 15

Jacob, My Spirit Guide

I was no stranger to the hospital waiting room. My father had catheterizations, stents, bypasses, open heart surgeries, mitral valve replacement and a defibrillator installed over the course of the last forty years of his life. So, once again, I found myself waiting for hours and praying fervently for my father to survive another heart procedure.

At this point in my life, I had been providing psychic tarot card readings at events and for private clients. As my readings became increasingly accurate, I also started to hear the names of people that were deceased. I realized my clairaudience ability was becoming stronger like when I was a small child, prompting me to explore mediumship development classes. In 2014, I began attending a mediumship practice circle at a local spiritual center and started taking classes. As I sat waiting in the hospital to hear news about my father's surgery, I attempted to distract myself by reading a book for beginners that offered guidance on how to meet and connect with your Spirit Guides.

I closed my eyes and took deep breaths to try and quiet my mind and then followed the instructions on how to go about meeting my Spirit Guides. I imagined myself walking along a beautiful forest path adorned on both sides with vibrant flowers and lush trees. Birds were singing, and the golden sun was shining in a perfect blue sky. I walked for a bit and continued to take in the beautiful scenery, scents, and sounds, all while continuing to focus on my breathing. Eventually the path began to wind, and the trees grew extremely dense to the point that they blocked my path, leaving only a small opening which I proceeded to go through. Suddenly, the scenery changed, and I found myself in a vast desert. I began trudging through the sand, shielding my eyes from the bright hot sun. There was nothing around me but sand so I continued to walk until I could see tents in the distance. I could sense someone coming towards me and he appeared a short distance in front of me.

The stranger motioned for me to walk towards him and so I did his bidding while he waited for me to come closer. I could see every feature in his wise elderly face that was sun-tanned and almost leathered with age. His high forehead was deeply wrinkled and covered with age spots, and his long hair and beard were silvery white with sparse strands of its original dark color. The stranger wore a long white tunic cinched with what looked like a leather rope, he carried a wooden staff, and his feet were adorned with simple sandals. He smiled and extended both of his thin arms out to me in a welcoming gesture, and then hugged me close. I could see the depths of wisdom in his twinkling eyes. "Welcome," the stranger said, "My name is Jacob and I have been waiting for you as long as the stars have been in the Heavens." I did not understand what Jacob meant by that statement and then he placed his hand on my shoulder, smiled and said, "Do not worry, it is not your father's time yet," and I instantly felt relieved and comforted. Then an announcement came over the hospital intercom system startling me out of my meditative state and bringing me back to reality.

It is hard to describe what I felt in that moment realizing I had met Jacob from the Bible. Besides feeling overwhelmed at the thought that Jacob was my Spirit Guide, every fiber of my being tingled with this energy that resonated with feelings of love, guidance, comfort, and wisdom. As I digested this experience, my father's surgeon appeared and confirmed Jacob's message stating that the procedure went well, and my father was in recovery.

Jacob is my Master Spirit Guide who keeps me on my spiritual path of enlightenment. Over the years, through subsequent meditations, I also have come to know and rely on two of my other main guides, one being a Buddhist monk who acts as my teacher, and the other is an American Indian who is my physical and spiritual protector. They have shared their names with me, and I recognize them by their images or how their energy feels. I rely on these three main guides as my Spirit Team for spiritual direction and guidance on all matters. I do have other Spirit Guides that I see, hear, or feel but I do not know their actual names, which is quite common, as we all have a team of Spirit Guides or Team of Light.

Clients often ask me during their reading sessions to tell them who their Spirit Guides are. I feel that discovering your guides and what they mean to you is personal and part of your spiritual growth and journey. It should be something that you learn on your own, through meditation, reflection, and prayer. You may go your whole life without knowing your Spirit Guide's true name. They may show you a symbol or "calling card" or you may just recognize their energy when they come close to you and that is common and perfectly fine. Feel free to give your guide a name that has meaning to you if they don't share their name with you. A Spirit Guide's true name should not matter, but rather you should focus on the guidance you are given and strive to maintain a steady and open link of communication with them to stay on the path of enlightenment and your soul's true destiny.

CHAPTER 16

I am a Medium

My earlier days of instruction on how to become a medium were mostly confusing and quite frustrating. I sat in practice circles with other aspiring mediums as we took turns attempting to connect with Spirit and relay messages to one another. Mostly the messages relayed from others talked about fairies or vague cryptic references that left much to the imagination. I was not hearing enough evidential information to be convinced that people were giving or receiving authentic messages from deceased loved ones. but I also knew that I should not have such elevated expectations since we were all beginners and learning.

In the beginning, the guidance I received to make a connection to Spirit was very methodical and rigid. I received instructions to start my mediumship sessions with the Prayer of Saint Francis. I am not sure why it had to be that specific prayer, because although lovely, it had no personal relevance or meaning for me. After reciting the prayer, I was then supposed to call upon my Joy Guide who functioned as the "gatekeeper" of spirit communication and controlled which Spirits would come in for the reading. None of this resonated with me or actually worked, and this ineffective process only served to fuel my frustration. I was quickly becoming disenchanted with the idea of wanting to be a medium, thinking that I just wasn't cut out for this path.

I had not yet encountered a medium that truly embodied the perception of what I thought a medium should be. I wanted to be wowed with hard cold facts as evidence from the Afterlife. I needed to be convinced that the discarnate soul the medium said they were communicating with was without a doubt them, and I needed to see the healing aspect of the relayed information on the faces of the those receiving messages. Nevertheless, I am not a quitter and so I continued to participate in mediumship classes and circles hoping to see improvement in my mediumistic ability.

After two more years of practicing, I was still not at the level of mediumship proficiency that I had hoped to achieve, nor had I found a role model teacher that could provide what I was looking for. Frustrated in having put in the time and effort, and not having much to show for it, I became skeptical about the whole medium concept and revisited the idea of walking away.

It was now January 2017, and I needed to decide if I was going to start the new year with pursuing mediumship or giving it up. I was leaning towards giving it up and that is when I received an advertisement email from a local venue regarding an upcoming mediumship event and classes being provided by a visiting New Jersey-based medium. I researched the advertised medium and became intrigued with her story and credentials, prompting me to sign up for both the evening demonstration and the mediumship development classes that were offered throughout the weekend.

I honestly believe that the Universe put this special woman in my path to change my perception about mediums and to reinforce my desire to pursue mediumship development. That evening during the demonstration of mediumship event, I watched with awe and admiration as Janet Nohavec delivered one highly evidential and impactful message after another. Janet, I learned, was a former Catholic nun, teacher, pastor, and founder of The Journey Within, A Center for Spiritual Evolvement in Northern

New Jersey. All I could think of while watching and listening to her demonstrate, was that this is what or who I was looking for. Janet delivered detailed and heartfelt messages of hope, healing and love as the audience members wept and laughed. She rekindled that desire in my soul to pursue mediumship and inspired me to develop into becoming a credible medium. I began training with her the very next day.

Under Janet's tutelage, I learned to communicate directly with discarnate spirits versus going through a third party like a Spirit Guide. I was taught to enable spirit communication in the way that was most comfortable for me, using the clairs that came naturally to me, rather than strict rules previously imposed on me confining me to one method. I was given permission and encouraged to prepare for readings using meditations, prayers, songs, or whatever method worked best to quiet my mind and allow me to sit in the power and enable spirit communication. I continued to take about a dozen classes with Janet and other teachers affiliated with The Journey Within and eventually joined Janet's advanced medium practice group. I was doing the work to grow spiritually and professionally as a credible medium and with the proper instruction and practice, my connection with Spirit and mediumship proficiency became strong.

Janet transitioned into Spirit in July 2022, and I am sad that I never had the chance to get to know her on a personal level, but only as a revered teacher. I was just one of many students that Janet unknowingly inspired to be of service on behalf of Spirit and those who are experiencing grief from the loss of a loved one. She stressed the importance of recognizing the responsibility of a medium to adhere to a higher level of morality, ethics, and respect through the delivery of quality, meaningful and evidential mediumistic readings. Janet not only ignited the spark inside of me to become an evidential medium, but she also provided the tools and training I needed to keep me aligned to my soul's true purpose and path of enlightenment.

I was no longer confused and finally understood that I was a natural born medium. This clarity brought joy to my soul as I finally recognized my true destiny, but even though I was eager and committed to pursuing this path, I was not free to do so yet. I still had to manage my full-time job, family obligations and overcome my own reservations that lingered about the capacity of my abilities. All these factors required my time and energy, prohibiting me from focusing on personal growth and pursuing my psychic mediumship business. With that being said, I transitioned from The Confused Soulitude to The Compromised Soulitude.

CHAPTER 17

White Noise Vibration

I first became aware of the strange white noise vibration during my episodes of sleep paralysis that followed my Life Review (first near-death experience). White noise was also present during my second and third near-death experiences as well as being a standard component of my intense flying dreams. During all these instances, I was in an altered state of consciousness which facilitated the higher vibrational connection to the Spirit World.

There has been only one instance to date that I experienced the familiar white noise vibration while being fully aware and conscious…it happened in the early morning hours of April 12, 2017. I was not surprised, and in fact knew for certain that the foreboding call would come this day based on the continual signs I had been receiving from Spirit, so I had prepared for it as best as I could. I will relay the details and story of these signs separately in the next chapter entitled "444".

I hung up the phone with my mother who had just given me the news that my father had transitioned into Spirit. I was dealing with a mixed bag of emotions as I was grateful for my father's suffering to end but of course, I was already painfully missing his physical presence. I showered, gathered my wits about me and got into my car to head toward my parents' home to offer what comfort I could to my mother and proceed with making all the necessary arrangements pertaining to my father's death. As I settled into the driver's seat, I said aloud "Dad, you know you can talk to me, please let me know you can hear me." I proceeded to turn on the ignition and the radio came on automatically belting the words "I hear your voice, it's like an angel sighing, I have no choice, I hear your voice," from the popular Madonna song *Like a Prayer*. I broke down in tears from receiving that powerful confirmation from my father through the words of a song.

If a medium ever brought through my father for me during a reading session and said the name "Madonna" it would truly be relevant in pertaining to that powerful message. There are also two other reasons that name is significant for me. First, Madonna was one of my favorite singers during high school and I was always blasting her records and singing along very loudly in my bedroom which annoyed my parents and the neighbors. I'm also embarrassed to admit to going through a brief phase where I dressed like the pop icon in mostly black attire, wearing a big cross earring and sporting the big bow in my hair. The second reason is that there is a funny reference to "Madonna" from my early childhood memories of my father and it is one of my favorite stories to tell.

As mentioned previously, my father had a thick Italian accent and would consistently butcher the English language which often made us laugh. We were not necessarily laughing at him, but the way he mixed up or pronounced certain words often resulted in hilarity. When I was a little girl, my father liked to sing nursery rhymes to me both in Italian and in English.

One day in kindergarten, the teacher asked for a volunteer to recite or sing their favorite nursery rhyme and I volunteered. I made my way to the front of the class and started to sing my favorite nursery rhyme that my father had taught me. I only belted the first sentence out "Oh Madonna had a farm, Hee, Hi, Hee Hi Ho!" when everyone in the class burst out laughing. For the life of me I had no idea what was so funny and began to wonder if it was my singing voice that the other children were making fun of. I was fighting back the tears as my teacher quickly admonished my classmates and told them to be quiet. She then gently approached me and informed me that I was singing the lyrics incorrectly. I looked at her in disbelief and then watched and listened silently in horror as my teacher proceeded to sing and then the rest of the class joined in singing the correct version of Old MacDonald had a Farm.

It was torture getting through the rest of the day enduring the smirks and jeers from my classmates and by the time I got home, my humiliation had turned to anger. I confronted my mother demanding to know why my father taught me a version of the nursery rhyme having the blessed Virgin Mary as the proprietor of the farm with all the animals. My mother just gave me an exasperated look and tried to explain as best as she could that sometimes my father pronounced things differently because he came from another country. She then suggested that the next time I volunteered for this school activity that I should sing one of the Italian nursery rhymes my father taught me because it would impress my classmates. There was no way I was doing this as my young mind had quickly learned that anything that sounded different would surely be ridiculed by my classmates. Instead, I decided to forego this activity going forward and keep quiet in class. Thank goodness I was already following my intuition at such an early age, because my second favorite nursey rhyme was "Tinkle, Tinkle, Lulu Star." So, you can see the name "Madonna" has a lot of relevance to me.

It took me a few minutes to regain my composure from the emotional effect of this much needed sign that came from my father via a song on the radio and then I pulled out of the garage and started down the driveway. I decided to check the mailbox which had been neglected for the past few days since I was spending so much time at my parents' house. As I quickly sorted through the mail to make sure there was nothing that needed my immediate attention, I found myself staring incredulously at a letter from an organization called the "Salvatorian Society." I had never heard of this society before nor did I ever receive mail from them, but I know that it was another powerful sign from my father, as his name was Salvatore. I felt enormous gratitude having received two powerful signs from my father within minutes of each other and in such a brief time since he passed, and this made me smile through my tears.

The Latin phrase "Omen trium perfectum" translates to "everything that comes in threes is perfect," and my father still had one more powerful sign to send me that day to make my day perfect. As I made my way to my parents' house, I phoned my good friend, Andrea, to relay the news of my father's passing. We spoke for a couple of minutes and then something strange started happening. I began to hear static and then a high-pitched noise came through the blue tooth car stereo connected to my iPhone. "Andrea, can you hear me?" I kept asking over the static, but my friend did not reply. The static crackling and high-pitched sound intensified, and I suddenly felt like my lungs had filled up with air and were about to burst. I pulled over to the side of the road and then exhaled so hard as if I had been holding my breath for several minutes. The static and high-pitched noise from the car radio stopped and became replaced with that familiar white noise humming vibration. It took over my being and left me with a sense of calm and peacefulness. Then, I felt an incredible and powerful rush of love from my father come over me and I knew that he was at peace and still with me.

This was the only time to date that I have experienced the white noise vibration in a state of awareness, and I knew instantly that my soul had blended with my father's soul for a brief moment to experience that powerful exchange of pure love.

CHAPTER 18

444

Throughout my life, I have often heard people talk about signs and symbols they have received from their loved ones that have passed on. Of course, I knew this to be common and absolutely believed that these people were having meaningful experiences with signs and symbols from the deceased, but I had not yet had a spiritual sign experience of my own because I had not experienced the loss of someone close to me.

I found it strange and quite frankly, a little uncomfortable to talk knowingly about this subject with my clients as a practicing psychic medium without having a real-life applicable frame of reference.

This all changed for me in the early morning hours of September 17, 2016, at 4:44 AM. I was in a hotel room in Jacksonville, Florida, with my father who had accompanied me on this trip to see my son, Nicholas, receive an academic award from the college he was attending. As a single mother, my father was very instrumental in helping me raise my two sons and I thought he would enjoy seeing a college campus to gain an understanding of what his first grandson was accomplishing coming from a poor upbringing in Calabria, Italy, which only afforded him a fourth-grade education. Excited to see Nicholas and start the day's planned family activities, I woke up early to see the bright red glaring numbers of 4:44 am on the digital clock on the nightstand adjacent to my bed. For a second, I thought it strange to see the sequence of numbers but quickly dismissed it and hopped out of bed to shower and get ready for the day. I had no idea that this was the beginning of seven months of a continual barrage of seeing 444 everywhere, nor did I understand the huge and significant impact those numbers would have on my life.

As the days and weeks passed by, I received frequent signs of 444 in a variety of ways. I would wake up at least once a week at exactly 4:44 AM. I received receipts, tickets, phone calls and texts with the numbers 444 imbedded in them somehow. I saw street signs, advertisements, billboards, license plates, mileage numbers, GPS arrival times, and much more with 444. It was everywhere and honestly sometimes obnoxiously in my face and so I started journaling the occurrences and making notes.

I knew of Angel Numbers and researched 444 learning that this sequence of numbers meant that you have nothing to fear as Angels are surrounding, loving, and guiding you on the right path. This was very enlightening and encouraging as I was evolving spiritually, but intuitively I knew that this was not just about me and that the 444 sign was directly connected to my father. I did not think it was a coincidence that it started when I was alone with him on that trip to Jacksonville. In November 2016, I made this journal entry "4 = the month of April and 4+4+4 = 12. What is the significance of April 12th?"

My father was, without a doubt, the strongest person I have ever known. His will to live and push on despite a failing heart was unbelievable! At the age of forty-two my father underwent open-heart surgery after a sudden heart attack caused by blockage in the three main arteries. In his mid-seventies he had another open-heart surgery, followed by stents and a defibrillator installed. Despite unfavorable odds and to the amazement of his team of medical doctors, my father's surgeries were all successful, giving him more time here. My father refused to give in to his coronary artery disease and bradycardia and was always on the move, whether it be gardening, walking around farmer's markets to buy fresh fruits and vegetables or watching his grandsons' football games and practices, cheering them on from the bleachers even though he really did not understand the game. He loved to be involved and active but despite his strong will, his body finally began to fail him.

In January and February 2017, my father was in and out of the hospital due to his defibrillator firing off as his heart became weaker and weaker. I knew it was not looking good and had to come to terms with the fact that this seemingly invincible man was fading rapidly in front of my very eyes. I phoned his remaining siblings and nephew that he was especially close with in New York, letting them know that I did not think my father had much more time left in this world. I suggested that they may want to visit him in Florida soon. By this time, I had come to accept what my soul already knew and what my Spirit Team was conveying with the 444 signs—my father would pass on April 12th.

By March 2017, my father's constitution had become so frail that he mostly slept, and it was necessary to transport him around by wheelchair. The strong man that was always laughing, joking, and smiling looked so sad and tired now. It made my heart break as I knew he was ready to go. In late March, his brother, sisters, and nephew came to visit him for a long weekend and to inevitably say their goodbyes. It seemed as if my father had reserved the remnants of his strength for those couple of days with his family as he rallied just enough for them to take him out to have dinner at a restaurant on the water. My father always loved the beach, and I was so grateful to have the help of my cousin who wheeled him out to the beach on Anna Maria Island where he enjoyed the warmth of the sun on him. It was the first time in weeks that I saw him smile and I was so grateful that his family came to show their love and support for him.

Monday morning came far too quickly, and it was time for my relatives to head back to New York. I woke up incredibly early and went into my office to check on the status of their flights. I turned on my laptop and as my home screen with the digital clock came up, it displayed 4:44 AM in big bold numbers and at that exact time, the power went off for a couple of seconds in my entire house! I just stood there, frozen while my husband, Nick, yelled out from our bedroom "the power turned off at 4:44!". My Aunt came out from the guest bedroom and just gave me a bewildered look. I had told her about the 444 experiences and now she too witnessed the alarm clock in the guest bedroom still flashing 4:44 from when the power went off. It was all very overwhelming and a bit eerie.

The goodbyes were especially hard for my relatives because of knowing they would not see my father again. My father transitioned to hospice care the day after his family left. As I outlined the desired nursing care schedule with the hospice nurse, she began to plan out the month of April. I let her know that my father would be passing on April 12th due to signs that I had received from Spirit to which she nodded her head in a polite acknowledgement while the look on her face said, "you are batshit crazy". I had become used to other people that did not understand psychic abilities or my connection to Spirit thinking that I was out of my mind, so I ignored the look. Even my own mother thought I was crazy to assume that I could know so far in advance the exact day that my father would pass.

The next day, I went to spend time with my father and took him outside in the wheelchair so he could enjoy the fresh air. My mother was battling lung cancer and was unsteady on her feet and unable to maneuver the wheelchair safely for either of them, so my father was grateful for my visits. I was about to pull up to the guard entrance to give the required information for entry when a car abruptly pulled in front of me exposing the license plate in plain view with 444 as the center numbers and simultaneously the radio started playing "My Old Man" by the Zach Brown band. I burst into tears; April 12th was just three days away.

I was not surprised when the inevitable phone call came from my mother in the early morning of April 12, 2017, letting me know my father had transitioned into Spirit, as I was expecting it. My father continues to send the 444 signs letting us know he is still very much present in our lives. I typically see the special 444 sign when I am thinking about him or asking for guidance. I know that my father is protecting me and my family from the Other Side and the most memorable evidence of this belief happened a couple of months after he had passed.

One afternoon, my husband Nick and I decided to go out spontaneously for a quick bite to eat. We headed towards Sarasota, Florida, and were driving on a four-lane highway at about forty miles an hour when suddenly the cars in front of us in both the left and right lanes decided to switch to our lane simultaneously. The two cars swerved in front of us from opposite sides of our truck. Nick, who was driving, yelled out "Hold on!" and I braced myself for what was sure to be a collision. Everything happened so quickly and as I closed my eyes anticipating the hit, I saw my father's face smiling at me. When I opened my eyes seconds later, everything was fine. "What happened?" I asked my husband incredulously. Nick, visibly shaken, just shook his head and said "I cannot explain it. We should have collided with both cars but somehow everyone moved the right way at the right time and avoided a terrible and possibly fatal accident." We now were stopped at a traffic light, and I told my husband that when I had closed my eyes bracing for the impact, I saw my father's face. We both agreed that he was looking out for us from the Other Side and then the car to the right of us switched over to the far-right lane and the car behind it moved forward in front of us revealing the license plate with 444 on it! My husband and I just looked at each other and knew without a doubt that my father had helped us to avoid a major accident.

Now, I want to be perfectly clear in stating that seeing sequential numbers or other signs are not meant to be interpreted as foreseeing someone's death. I do not believe that anyone has the power to predict the day of death as that is something that only our Creator knows. Signs from our deceased loved ones are always positive and loving in nature and are meant to give us comfort. I will expand a little more about signs in the next chapter.

For me, 444, was a gift from the Universe telling me the exact day of my father's passing so that I could plan and make the best use of my father's final days and contact his family to give them the opportunity to spend time with him before he transitioned to Spirit. It was only my heightened sense of intuition that enabled me to know that this 444 Angel sign was also a special connection to the day of my father's passing.

CHAPTER 19

Forever Family Foundation

I first became aware of Forever Family Foundation in the Fall of 2018. I was still in The Compromised Soulitude managing a full-time job and family responsibilities that kept me from devoting a substantial portion of my time to pursue mediumship, but I was doing the best that I could to find time to develop my mediumship abilities. A dear friend that I met through a mediumship development class introduced me to Forever Family Foundation and invited me to join her at an Afterlife Explorers and Mediumship Convention in Fort Myers, Florida, in November 2018. I was intrigued and accepted her invitation.

The conference provided presentations and workshops by certified Forever Family Foundation mediums as well as other contributing professionals and authors lecturing about near-death experiences, paranormal phenomena and other evidence and education proving that once we leave our physical bodies, we absolutely do survive physical death.

I had the opportunity to meet the wonderful Forever Family Foundation founders, Bob and Phran Ginsberg, and learn their story and purpose behind starting this organization in 2004. Forever Family Foundation is a federal 501C, not for profit organization, which runs solely on volunteer power. The foundation seeks to blur the lines between science and spirituality, focusing on providing evidence that we survive physical death. They provide a forum of support for individuals and families who have suffered the loss of a loved one including state-of-the-art information and services and ongoing research into the survival of consciousness and Afterlife Science. To assist in grief and loss, Forever Family Foundation established a Medium Evaluation Certification Process to offer a list of vetted mediums as resources in healing for the bereaved. This certification process is a science-based examination of the ability of a specific medium to bring forth information without the use of fraudulent or deceptive means. Under controlled conditions, the evidence communicated by mediums gets evaluated and scored, and only those exhibiting a high degree of accuracy and consistency are granted certification. It is worth noting that approximately 85% of the mediums evaluated will fail to meet the minimum requirements for the certification.

Throughout the weekend, I attended various informational and fun workshops and lectures on spirit communication, spoon bending, deathbed visions, ghosts, and hauntings. At the close of the convention's weekend events, there was an opportunity for aspiring mediums to participate in an event called "strut your stuff" where they could give messages to the audience of conference attendees which would be judged by a panel of Forever Family Foundation certified mediums. I had never given a group reading before so naturally I was extremely nervous and intimidated, but the opportunity to demonstrate in front of reputable authentic mediums and receive their guidance and constructive criticism on how I can improve my mediumship skills was very appealing to me and so I went for it. The overall feedback I received from the panel was that my evidence was decent, and my style of delivery and personality was commendable, and they encouraged me to keep working at it. I took this feedback to heart and left the conference inspired by Forever Family Foundation and the kind and compassionate people that I had interacted with dedicated to the organization's mission of providing support for the bereaved and providing evidence that there is indeed an Afterlife.

I knew I wanted to be a part of this organization and part of the comfort and healing they provided for the bereaved through vetted authentic mediums. I set a personal goal to do the work necessary in developing my mediumship abilities so that I could become one of their certified mediums.

For the next two and a half years, I pushed myself working a full-time job, handling family obligations, and providing twenty to thirty readings a month plus I started giving small group demonstrations at local venues and in private homes on the evenings and weekends. In time, I had succeeded in establishing myself as an authentic medium and continuing to do the group demonstrations had afforded me comfortability and ease with presenting in front of audiences. In fact, to my surprise, the group demonstrations became the most enjoyable for me. Despite being exhausted from trying to balance all the aspects of my life due to being in The Compromised Soulitude, I intuitively knew that being a medium was my soul's true destiny, so I kept pushing forward. I was receiving constant positive feedback and validation from my clients, but it was not enough for me. Even though my soul knew I was a credible medium, I was experiencing self-doubt about my abilities, another trait of being in The Compromised Soulitude, and needed more affirmation. I wanted to get certified by an organization known for vetting authentic mediums and after putting in the work, I felt ready to begin the Medium Evaluation Certification process with Forever Family Foundation.

I remember crying tears of joy and great relief as I read the email dated April 22, 2021, from Bob Ginsberg, congratulating me on achieving the required level of proficiency to become one of Forever Family Foundation's certified mediums. I had set a personal goal and achieved it! This validation enabled me to discard any self-doubt or reservations about my mediumistic abilities and my soul's true calling. It felt like a huge weight had been lifted off my shoulders knowing all my hard work and dedication had paid off. I began volunteering my time with this wonderful organization and contributing my spiritual gifts towards healing from grief and loss at various Grief Retreats held in California, Connecticut and Florida and making guest appearances on Signs of Life Radio providing live readings on the air.

Obtaining the Forever Family Foundation Medium Certification gave me the validation I needed to transition partially into The Clear Soulitude, truly knowing and accepting my soul's destiny, but I still lingered in The Compromised Soulitude because of my other full-time work obligation. Determined to do what makes my soul happy, I began working towards another personal goal of being able to devote myself full-time to my psychic mediumship practice.

CHAPTER 20

Signs

Signs from our loved ones in Spirit are everywhere, we just need to be open to receiving them, and not putting too many boundaries or restrictions on what they are, when we should receive them or the way in which they should be presented to us. In other words, breathe, let it go, and do not put demands on or try to control the Spirit World. Just as mediums do not control which Spirits come through in a reading, we also do not control the Spirit World when it comes to the signs we expect to receive from them.

If I had a nickel for every time a client asked me during their reading what sign they should be looking for from their loved one that had transitioned, I would be very wealthy. Now do not get me wrong, Spirits do come through in readings and show me a specific bird, or a butterfly, turtle, flower, or other symbol, letting me know that it was indeed them sending a sign to my client. Sometimes Spirit gives a sign for my clients to watch out for in the future and I have received positive feedback after these readings from my clients validating that they did in fact receive that specific sign mentioned during their reading. I also have been known to receive the special "code word" that was set up between a client and their loved one before they passed as definitive proof that they are truly still around.

You may have a special sign that has meaning for you and somehow connects to your deceased loved one, like the 444 sign connects to my father for me. But what if you do not have a special sign? How do you know what to look for? This was exactly the situation I found myself in when my mother passed. I did not know what sign to expect from her as there was nothing that had special meaning to me prior to her passing and we did not set up a code word. I have to say that I felt bad about this since the 444 sign was so prominent and meaningful for my father.

Often we are so focused on one specific sign that we are looking and hoping for that we miss the other signs that our loved ones are sending us. It is a good thing to put your intentions out to your deceased loved ones and ask for a specific sign from them, but I also believe that it is best not to make looking for the sign a full-time job which will lead to stress and disappointment when you don't receive it right away. Remember, we do not control it—Spirit does! You will receive your sign in time, but you need to have patience and wait for it to happen organically. Remember signs can come in a variety of forms, for instance, you may ask Spirit to show you a turtle and so you keep your eyes peeled for a live turtle to cross your path. Instead of a live turtle, Spirit may send you the turtle sign in the form of a picture, a piece of clothing, stuffed animal, statue, etc., so keep your mind open. Also, I highly recommend being practical with your choice of signs. To put this in perspective, if someone asked you to find them a pink unicorn that had green eyes, a rainbow-colored mane wearing a purple tutu and white cowboy boots…how quickly do you think you could find one?

My mother was the most technically challenged person that I knew. She was the annoying customer that frequently called the cable company needing assistance in getting the television remote to work. She constantly had issues with her flip top phone and didn't understand how to read the messages or get her voicemail. My mother spoke to a customer service person from her bank at least twice a month because she consistently had issues accessing the online banking application and didn't understand how to pay her bills. Most troubling was that despite my constant warnings and admonishing, my mother continued to call strangers with heavy foreign accents when she received an error message on her laptop directing her to call an unknown number immediately to fix an issue. She was every computer hacker's dream, so I was really taken by surprise when the first sign that I received from my mother came in the form of technology…through my iPhone to be exact.

It happened in the middle of November 2022, about a week after my mother's passing. I was at her apartment cleaning up and organizing items to be donated to Good Will. I stopped to take a break to call Best Buy customer service because I had a gift card that I wanted to use to purchase Christmas gifts for the upcoming Black Friday specials. When I peeled back the film covering the pin code on the back of the gift card, a couple of the numbers rubbed off, so I had no idea what they were and couldn't use the gift card. I had been holding the line for about twenty minutes listening to elevator music when a customer service representative finally answered. I relayed the pin code problem and was returned to hold again while the representative researched the issue. I set my iPhone down in speaker mode on the dining room table and continued to clean and organize while I waited. Another ten minutes went by as the elevator music played on and on and then suddenly the music stopped, and I clearly heard "Welcome to Life Alert" and then the representative returned to the line. This was very strange because one of the last things I did about a month before my mother passed was to arrange for the Life Alert system to be installed in her apartment. In fact, earlier that very morning, the Life Alert company representative came to pick up the equipment that was no longer needed. Curious, I asked the Best Buy customer service representative about the random Life

Alert infomercial that I just heard before he came back on the line. The representative stated that they did not have commercials on hold, only music!

Could this really have happened or was my mind playing tricks on me? Despite being a medium and knowing full well this was in fact a real possibility as Spirit can manipulate electronics, I was still doubting this was a sign from my mother and thought it was just a fluky coincidence, but my mind would be changed a couple of months later.

It was the middle of January 2023, and I was still coping with the loss of my mother right before the Thanksgiving and the Christmas holidays. Determined to fulfill my resolution of spending more time with family, I called Air Canada to make the flight reservations for a family cruise in May that I had just finished booking. I had been on hold listening to the music for about ten minutes when unexpectedly I heard "Welcome to Life Alert" and then the Air Canda customer service representative came back on the line. Of course, I asked her about the infomercial I clearly heard while on hold and she confirmed that there were no commercials, only music on hold. Now that I experienced this message a second time, I was convinced that my mother was indeed trying to communicate with me via the Life Alert sign. To date, I have not experienced the phone infomercial again, but I do see Life Alert billboard advertisements and television commercials at certain times when I am thinking about my mother and know that this is one of the signs that she chose to give me.

A couple of months later, I ventured out to Brooksville, Florida, to do a private home demonstration at my Uncle Fran and Aunt Maureen's Florida residence. I was excited to do a mediumship event for a family member because the only person in my family who has seen me demonstrate is my husband, Nick. This is something that will always make me sad because I wish my parents could have seen me doing the work that I do to help those that are grieving, but I take comfort knowing they are watching from where they are now. I had two hours of driving time before reaching my destination and I began thinking about my mother. This would be the first time seeing members of her family since she passed. I put out an intention for my mother to give me a sign to show that she was with me. I specifically asked to see her name spelled out exactly the way she spelled it, "Marianne." Naturally, all the way to Brooksville, my eyes were searching the street signs, building signs and billboards hoping to see her name. I did not receive the sign I asked for during the drive there, my stay in Brooksville, or on the way back home leaving me sad and disappointed.

The day after I returned home, my son Anthony called to ask if I had a carry-on luggage bag that he could use for our upcoming trip in May. I did not have an extra one but remembered that I had grabbed a couple of large suitcases from my mother's apartment when I was cleaning it out. I had shoved the suitcases into the back of the spare bedroom closet and never bothered to look to see if anything was inside of them. I pulled the first one out and inside of it was a medium-sized suitcase. I pulled the second suitcase out and inside of it I discovered a small carry-on suitcase that would be perfect for my son. I unzipped the carry-on and found a hot pink luggage strap with the words "BON VOYAGE" printed across the front side and when I lifted it out of the carry-on, the back side of the strap revealed my mother's name in big bold letters "MARIANNE.'

This blew my mind, not only had I received the specific sign of my mother's name that I had asked for, but the words "BON VOYAGE" were also meaningful as I sensed my mother was letting us know that she was aware of our upcoming family trip that we were leaving for on Mother's Day. I continue to see my mother's name in random places and hear her name in songs that I have never heard before.

I have learned two important things about signs from our loved ones in Spirit; the first is that they control the what, whens, wheres and how we receive them, and the second is that we can also put our intentions out to the Spirit World requesting a special sign. Both are meaningful and both prove that the bonds of love are eternal and that our loved ones are always with us.

CHAPTER 21

The Past, Present and Future Me

While receiving the download of content into my consciousness for this book, my Spirit Team promised that I would begin to understand my true self as I embarked on my writing journey. This was true as certain people, places and events did transpire bringing clarification about my connection to Isis, Egypt, and the Afterlife. The final event that took place to enable me to put the pieces of my life's puzzle together came through information gained via a past life regression session conducted in December 2023 by my friend and colleague, Jacob Cooper, LCSW.

I was excited about this session, having always wanted to experience a past life regression, but also felt a bit apprehensive knowing that it is not easy for me to quiet my mind for prolonged periods of time which would be ideal for a productive session. The meditation sessions I engage in before providing readings and performing events are typically short (about fifteen minutes). Through trial and error, I have learned that listening to upbeat music, walking in nature, or riding my bike are more effective ways to raise my vibration and better suited for my hyper personality versus the more customary practice of going into a deep meditative state.

My doubts quickly dissipated as Jacob began the session by making me feel comfortable and relaxed as he guided me into a state of relaxation, and it was not long in this altered state of consciousness before I met my deceased parents and dogs in the Afterlife bringing me immense joy. Jacob took me back farther into my past life experiences and suddenly a very vivid and detailed vision of a past life appeared in my mind as if I were watching a movie.

In this past life vision, I saw myself as a young boy around the age of six years old living in ancient Egypt in the times of the great Pharaohs and pyramids. I watched myself as this young boy attempting to sneak into a great pyramid palace trying to catch a glimpse of my father being aware that he was a member of the prestigious family that lived there. I also intuitively knew that this was something that I did often because my father was an absent figure in my life. I grew up without my father because he impregnated my mother when she worked as a handmaiden at the royal palace, to be cast out later when her pregnancy became revealed. Then my vision shifted to catch a glimpse of my mother carrying a woven basket filled with fruit. She was incredibly beautiful with large expressive almond-shaped eyes and long black hair that fell to her waistline. My vision focus shifted back to the task at hand of entering the pyramid. Two guards holding long spears and wearing metal helmets stood on either side of the pyramid entrance. When they became distracted, I was able to sneak past them and quickly ran down a corridor and then darted into one of the open rooms. As I glanced around the room, the first thing I noticed was a small three-tier round stone bathing pool. Right next to the stone pool, an enormous golden sculpture of a peacock with its feathers spread wide stood perched on top of a large stone pillar. The magnificent golden peacock sculpture was about six feet in both height and diameter, and its golden reflection appeared in the water of the stone pool. The finely etched details in the golden face and feathers of the peacock were breathtaking. I felt incredibly drawn to this sculpture as it seemed oddly familiar to me. Next, I heard voices coming from the corridor, so I quickly ran back outside, not wanting to be caught. I felt disappointed in not having been able to see my father but knew I would try again another day. When I came outside, my attention was immediately brought to the incredibly bright sun illuminating the sky behind the pyramids. Intuitively, I knew there was something important about the imagery of that sun and the golden peacock sculpture I had just encountered as the images kept flashing back and forth in my mind.

At this point in the vision, I heard Jacob's voice telling me to go a little bit farther in my past life timeline and my vision moved to when I was about fourteen years old. I was aware my mother had recently passed, leaving me an orphan. All alone in the world, I became a nomad and performed odd chores for food and shelter, relying on the kindness of strangers to survive.

Jacob prompted me to go further and now I saw myself as a young man. I was walking on foot through the desert lands just trying to survive. My travels eventually led to a settlement of people. I could smell food cooking over a campfire, and I walked hopefully towards the tents. As I got closer, an old man emerged from one of the tents and started walking towards me. As he drew closer, I became both excited and confused because I recognized this old man. He was my Master Spirit Guide, Jacob, from the Bible! This was very strange seeing him in a past life vision. Jacob welcomed me into his arms, and I felt safe and loved. I knew that I belonged there with Jacob and in that moment I had a revelation of clarity remembering when I first met Jacob over ten years ago while meditating in the hospital waiting room as my father underwent heart surgery. At that time Jacob greeted me with the words "I have been waiting for you as long as the stars have been in the Heavens." It all made sense to me now understanding that I shared a past life connection with Jacob my Master Spirit Guide and this insight was truly overwhelming.

As I continued further back in the past life regression, I saw that I assimilated into the tribe and a couple of years later, married a woman called Zara who shortly afterwards gave birth to a little girl. The last detail I remember is seeing men of the tribe pounding out and shaping thin pieces of some kind of metal to make jewelry and then my vision abruptly ended, and I returned to my normal waking state of mind.

I could not believe how clear and detailed this past life regression session was for me. There were so many images and details that stood out in my vision prompting a desire to do research to understand their true meaning. First, I wanted to understand what the peacock symbolized in the Egyptian belief system and in researching learned that in Egyptian mythology this bird reflected the earthly manifestations of the phoenix and symbolizes immortality and rebirth. The peacock is also linked to the worshipping of the god of the sun and sky, Horus, as Egyptians associated the large circle on the peacock's feather with the all-seeing Eye of Horus, a symbol of protection, healing, rebirth, wholeness, and knowledge. The images in my past life regression of the peacock and sun are intertwined with the association to Horus, who is the son of Isis, all representing psychic connection, rebirth, immortality, protection, healing, transformation, and spiritual awakening.

Now I understand why approximately a year prior to this past life regression session, I randomly had the urge to redecorate my home office where I conduct my readings and on-line training workshops. My home was just three years old at the time and my office decorations were fairly new, so there was no need to change anything, but for some reason I felt inspired to have a peacock-themed office. I purchased a bunch of peacock feathers which are arranged in a vase on a side table next to my reading chair that has a decorative pillow embellished with a large, beautiful, embroidered peacock. I also bought miscellaneous decorative items like an area rug, candles, artwork, and accent pillows for the sofa all in the bright colors of peacock teals, blues, and greens.

In May 2023 on the cruise where I started to draft this book, I visited a monastery on one of the islands in Greece where we encountered roaming wild peacocks. I remember feeling such a strong connection to those beautiful birds and spent the afternoon enjoying their peaceful company taking pictures of them roaming around the beautiful grounds. I also purchased different items decorated with the all-seeing Eye of Horus, including a zipped pouch for my tarot cards, a beach tote, bracelets, and coffee mugs.

As I was putting the finishing touches on the draft of this book, I reached back out to Dave Campbell, my Forever Family Foundation colleague who provided my astrological chart reading revealing the connection to Isis, to see if there was any other information I should include about my astrological chart. Upon reviewing my chart, Dave found that Juno, the goddess of marriage, who's totem animal is the peacock is very prominently placed in my chart being in conjunction with the Moon, thus revealing another predestined connection to the peacock.

The past life regression session and astrological chart findings brought me the understanding of why the peacock (which I now know is my spirit animal) and all-seeing eye of Horus, Isis and Egypt all resonate with me. But I remained perplexed about seeing my Master Spirit Guide Jacob, in my past life regression vision. I knew that Jacob settled in the land of Canaan which was in the territory of southern Levant (today this area encompasses modern Israel, Jordan, and Palestine), so I did not understand how I could have met him in Egypt. Curious, I researched Jacob's movements and learned in the latter part of his life, a famine prompted Jacob and his sons to move to Egypt, where he became reunited with his youngest son Joseph. Jacob lived in Egypt until his death.

My spiritual journey to find out everything about me, prompted me to get my DNA tested. As mentioned previously, my father was born in Calabria, Italy and my mother's grandparents were from that same region of Italy. I expected my DNA to come back ninety plus percent Italian as no other nationality was ever mentioned. Interesting enough, my DNA reveals that I am approximately 11% Egyptian and Levantine, further solidifying my connection to these areas.

I had finally come full circle in understanding the past, present and future me now understanding the connections to Isis, Horus, Jacob, Egypt, the peacock, and the Afterlife. From a very early age, my soul was guiding me to my true destiny of being a psychic medium and a bridge of communication and healing between the worlds of the living and the dead.

CHAPTER 22

Clear at Last

L ike everyone else, I came into this world a beautiful soul in The Clear Soulitude. At an incredibly young age, I was able to see and hear Spirit. As I grew older and became able to make my own choices and discern information, my spiritual journey led me to people, places and events that would shape my future and guide me on the path of enlightenment and my soul's true destiny.

I shifted from the Clear Soulitude and spent time in The Confused and The Closed Soulitudes where I learned valuable life lessons that enabled me to grow spiritually. I learned to recognize and accept the meaningful messages and signs that were being sent from The Universe and my soul in an effort to guide me to finding my soul's true purpose, but still remained in The Compromised Soulitude as I was unable to dedicate myself full-time to my spiritual psychic medium practice.

I knew it would take arduous work, focus, and sacrifice to reach this goal, but I was determined to move out of The Compromised Soulitude and back to The Clear Soulitude. I began ramping up the number of readings and events I performed every month to build my name recognition and clientele. The next couple of years were extremely challenging for me mentally, physically, and energetically as I worked vigorously towards my goal of freeing myself from my main employment.

Then in November 2023, something quite unexpected and wonderful happened. I received communication from my employer that they were offering an early retirement package for a select number of employees that met specific criteria and fortunately, I met that criteria! I genuinely believed that the Universe had bestowed an extraordinary gift signaling that without a doubt it was time for me to make a move. I accepted the early retirement offer without hesitation and left my full-time corporate position on January 1, 2024.

My soul was elated knowing I was finally able to live the life I was meant to live, working in the service of Spirit. I transitioned out of The Compromised Soulitude and progressed to The Clear Soulitude. I could now focus my time and energy on my psychic medium practice, providing messages of hope, healing, and love to those struggling with grief or in need of spiritual guidance.

As I drafted this very chapter, I received notification of successfully passing the Medium Certification process administered by Helping Parents Heal (HPH), a non-profit organization specifically dedicated to helping parents whose children have passed. This accomplishment is aligned with my spiritual progression and going forward, I hope to align myself with more like-minded individuals and organizations that advocate and support the bereaved and provide research and education regarding the existence of the Afterlife.

I intend to do everything in my power to remain in The Clear Soulitude and stay true to my soul's true destiny by sharing my knowledge of mediumship, near-death experiences, and the Afterlife through personal or group readings, mediumship training courses, and speaking at public events and conferences.

At last, I am aware of who I was, who I am, and my path is truly clear as to who I am supposed to be going forward. I know that my soul's destiny is to bring healing to those experiencing grief by being the bridge of communication between the physical and spiritual realms by providing evidential meaningful messages proving that there is an Afterlife and that the bonds of love are eternal and unbreakable.

I hope that in learning about The Soulitudes and my spiritual journey, that you can reflect on your own life experiences. Look back at the people that have crossed your path, the decisions you have made, and the events, challenges, and accomplishments that you have experienced and ask yourself, what made your soul happy? The answer to that question is how you will discover your soul's true destiny.

Always remember…You Are Soul Beautiful!

THE END

Epilogue

This is a truthful recollection of actual events in my life. Some conversations have been supplemented and/or recreated. The names and details of some people and organizations have been changed to protect their anonymity. The concepts and information provided about our souls, the Afterlife and the survival of consciousness are based on my own intuition, communication with my Spirit Team, and my first-hand spiritual and near-death experiences.

Acknowledgements

I am truly grateful for the love and support of my family and friends, both here and on the Other Side, who have helped this book come to fruition. In particular I would like to thank:

My husband Nick and our sons Nicholas and Anthony—I'm truly blessed to have such an amazing family. Thank you for all the love, patience, support and joy. You are my world!

Laura Lynne Jackson—Many heartfelt thanks for your evidential reading relaying details about this book coming to fruition, validating my own intuition in knowing that this book was part of my spiritual journey. www.lauralynnejackson.com

Bob Ginsberg—I am so very grateful to you for lending your support for this book as well as for all that you do through Forever Family Foundation in service of the bereaved and those seeking answers about the Afterlife. www.foreverfamilyfoundation.org

Dave Campbell—Thank you for your insightful astrological chart reading revealing my connection to Isis, the peacock, and the Afterlife. www.theastrologystore.com

Jacob Cooper, LCSW—Thank you for facilitating the past life regression session that brought clarity and further awareness of my soul's destiny. www.jacoblcooper.com

Tom and Melissa Gould—I am so grateful to you both for supporting this book through the gift of your extraordinary editing.

Carla Green—Thank you for bringing my book vision to life through your design and professional guidance. www.claritydesignworks.com

Psychic Andrea—I am so blessed and grateful to be able to call you my best friend. Thank you for your love, friendship, support, and guidance throughout the years as a treasured friend and amazing psychic. www.psychicsinthecity.com

About the Author

Connie Fusella is a natural born psychic medium with conscious memories of spirit communication beginning at the age of four. She has first-hand knowledge of the Afterlife through three near-death experiences which intensified her connection to the Other Side and led to her soul's true destiny of becoming a Psychic Medium.

Connie has proven and tested abilities to bridge the gap between the physical and spiritual realms and is an affiliated certified Medium with Helping Parents Heal (HPH) and Forever Family Foundation (FFF), which is featured on the Netflix series "Surviving Death." She is the award-winning author of *YOU ARE SOUL BEAUTIFUL A Unique Perspective into the Soul's Quest for Its Destiny*, the Recipient of the 2024 Speak Up Radio Firebird Award and 2024 Global Book Award. Connie has made several guest Medium appearances on *Signs of Life Radio*. Her clientele is worldwide, and she is available for private and group readings, fundraisers, public events, radio shows, grief retreats, and as a guest speaker on the topics of mediumship, NDEs or the Afterlife. She travels the country for events and works internationally via Zoom. Connie is a spiritual teacher and offers in-person and on-line mediumship training workshops.

Connie's compassionate demeanor, together with her exceptional accuracy, has resulted in a devoted international following and a reputation as one of the most trusted psychic mediums in the field. Through her experiences, work and gifts Connie consoles the bereaved and convinces the skeptics that there is an Afterlife, providing proof through evidential and heartfelt spirit communications that the bonds of love between our deceased loved ones and pets are eternal and unbreakable. She looks forward to sharing her gift and a meaningful message with you.

To schedule a reading or event,
or learn more about upcoming classes and events, visit:
www.meaningfulmessages.info

Follow Connie on social media:
Instagram: @psychicmediumconniefusella
Facebook: Meaningful Messages with Connie Fusella